CONTENTS.

	PAGE
Introduction	1
Hints to Young Housekeepers	6
Food and Diet	8
The Table	13
How to Cook	15
How to Clean Stoves and Cooking Utensils	19
Rules for Boiling	22
Rules for Roasting	23
Rules for Frying	24
Rules for Baking	26
Rules for Grilling	27
Rules for Broiling	27
Joints	28
Poultry and Game	32
Savoury Meat Dishes	40
Sauces	53
Breakfast Dishes and Beverages	69
Cold Meat Cookery	84
Entrées	92
Fish Cookery	111

INTRODUCTION.

THE importance of every woman having a thorough knowledge of domestic economy cannot be too strongly insisted on. The false refinement which, of late years, has considered an acquaintance with domestic matters to be only suitable for servants, has been fraught with the most disastrous consequences. This may seem strong language, but it is not too strong. All sanitary reformers know well enough that it is in the power of many women to prevent very many deaths, and an incalculable amount of misery and vice. Speaking of sanitary reform, the late Canon Kingsley says:—'Women can do in that work what men cannot. The private correspondence of women, private conversation, private example of ladies, above all of married women, of mothers of families, may do what no legislation can.' And again, in the same speech, delivered on behalf of the Ladies' Sanitary Association, he says: —'Ah! would to God that some man had the pictorial eloquence to put before the mothers of England the mass of preventable agony of mind and body which exists in England, year after year: and would that some man had the logical eloquence to make them understand that it is in their power, in the power of the mothers and wives of the higher classes—I will not say to stop it all, God only knows that—but to stop, as I believe, three-fourths of it.'

This may seem to some, perhaps, too serious an introduction to a cookery book; but it is my earnest wish that my book may not be simply a collection of recipes for cooks to refer to, but a real help to those women who, recognising the importance of good cookery in sanitary reform, are doing their utmost (as I know many are) to acquire that knowledge, and are thereby making the lives of those about them brighter and happier; and are also by their examples doing an amount of good that they themselves scarcely dream of. I have been told more than once by those benevolently interested in the working classes that with instruction to ladies on cookery they had no sympathy, and they seemed to think that it would be better if lessons on the subject were given exclusively to the poor. They forget that the wives of the working men are women who have most of them been domestic servants, and that what they learn in their situations, and what habits they there acquire, they take for *good* or *evil* into their own homes; and in this way an ignorant careless mistress may be doing an infinitude of harm to her sister women in a lower position than herself. On the other hand, a mistress who understands thoroughly the management of a house, by wisely training her servants in habits of order and industry, by teaching them what they do not know and have had no opportunity of learning about hygiene or the laws of health, may be—in fact cannot help being—a blessing indirectly to many homes.

I believe that the working classes must be taught in this way if they are to be taught at all. I have myself, over and over again, tried to benefit my poorer sisters by giving them free lessons on food and cookery; and although I invariably find a few who are very grateful for such instruction, the majority, I imagine, never trouble to put in practice what they have been taught. Their habits have been already formed, and it is not easy for them to alter them. But it is a significant fact that those who do value the lessons are generally respectable hardworking women, who have held good situations under good mistresses.

I have also heard it very ignorantly objected by some that by teaching ladies how to cook, you are taking the bread out of the servants' mouths. This is, indeed, the conclusion of a shallow mind; for with equal justice and good sense, it might be said that the owner of any large business was taking the bread out of his *employés'* mouths because he happened to be acquainted with all the details of his own business, and was able to see that those in his employment attended to their duties properly. But this, I suppose, everyone will admit, that the owner of any business ignorant of the management and details of it, would not unlikely one day find himself without any business to manage. And if this is true with regard to men's businesses, is it not equally so with regard to women's?

I have the greatest sympathy with servants, and would be the last to injure them in any way. A good servant is a treasure: and good work always deserves good wages. But the more a mistress knows of household work herself, the more is she likely to appreciate a servant who honestly and conscientiously performs her duties; and by understanding their difficulties, the more consideration is she likely to show to those in her employ.

But there are some ladies to whom a knowledge of domestic economy ought to be especially invaluable—namely, those whose means are so limited that they cannot afford to engage servants who have had any great experience, and, therefore, who keep only what is called a general servant, a term which often means a woman or girl who will undertake to do everything, but who has only the vaguest notions of how anything should be done. They, poor things, have had no opportunity of learning in the homes from which they came. But it will be well for the poor 'General' if her mistress can teach and train her; for she will then leave her situation with knowledge and habits that will make her a valuable and useful woman, and be of the greatest service to her all her life.

It is, however, quite surprising to see the rough way in which some people allow themselves to be served, and the muddle in which they prefer to live rather than do anything themselves that they consider menial; as if an untidy house, slovenly servants, badly cooked and coarsely served food, are not likely to do much more to lower their self-respect than any amount of so-called drudgery. 'A gentlewoman,' it has been said, 'never lowers herself by doing that which would make her feel less a gentlewoman if left undone.'

How much healthier and happier, too, many girls would be, if, instead of going out in all weathers, day after day, to earn a miserable pittance in any such employment as daily governesses, they would do some of the lighter housework, cooking, &c., at home. By being able to do with one servant instead of two, they would save probably more than they could earn in other ways, besides being much stronger from the exercise thus taken. But too many girls are, unfortunately, imbued with the vulgar notion that work is not genteel. What a Moloch this gentility has been and still is! What a number of human sacrifices are continually placed at its shrine, and what puppets its votaries become! Mr. Smiles says: 'There is a dreadful ambition abroad for being "genteel." We keep up appearances too often at the expense of honesty, and though we may not be rich, yet we must *seem* to be so. We must be "respectable," though only in the meanest sense—in mere vulgar outward show. We have not the courage to go patiently onward in the condition of life in which it has pleased God to call us, but must needs live in some fashionable state to which we ridiculously please to call ourselves; and all to gratify the vanity of that unsubstantial genteel world of which we form a part.'

It would effect a moral revolution if women would only look at matters in the true light. How much crime and misery may be traced to mismanaged unattractive homes! How many deaths to the ignorance of hygiene! How much intemperance to the physical depression caused by badly cooked food! Let us hope that the refinement, falsely so called, which is only another name for vanity, laziness, and selfishness, may soon give way to the true refinement of heart and mind which considers nothing too menial which will benefit others; nothing too common that will add to the happiness of our fellow-creatures.

If we women could earnestly and courageously endeavour to do the duty nearest to us, remembering that all honest work, of whatever kind, has been for ever ennobled by the great Founder of our Faith, so should we be, one in one way and one in another, 'helping to move (to quote Dean Goulburn) the wheels of the great world system whose revolutions are bringing on the kingdom of Christ.' 'To be good and to be useful,' as Canon Kingsley says, 'are the two objects for which we were sent into this world.'

HINTS TO YOUNG HOUSEKEEPERS.

> She looketh well to the ways of her household.
> *Proverbs of Solomon.*

TAKE care that you know definitely what sum you can afford to spend on your household expenses, and make it a point of conscience never to exceed it. Market with ready money, if possible; but, if it is more convenient to pay by the month, or quarter, never make that an excuse for letting your bills mount up to double what you can afford to pay. With accounts, carefully kept, it is quite possible to regulate the expenditure to the income.

Never order things at random, but inquire the price of everything before purchasing. Take every pains to know how to judge of the quality of meat, groceries, &c., so that you may not be imposed on. Never be ashamed to say you cannot afford to have this or that. To be poor may be a misfortune, but it is not a fault; and, indeed, to be rich is often a far greater misfortune. The discipline of poverty, and the self-denial it involves, will often strengthen a character which the luxury of riches would enervate.

Cultivate sufficient independence of character to enable you to form your household, and regulate your expenses according to your *own* means, and not according to the income of your neighbours. What does it matter if some may sneer at your thread-bare carpets and frugal fare? The approval of your own conscience is of far more importance than the friendship of the vulgar-minded. Above all things keep your accounts most strictly. Without this you are like a mariner without a compass, or chart, you don't know where you are or what is your position, and you will find yourself, before long, on the rocks of debt and difficulty. Extravagant housekeeping has been the cause of the most serious evils; and, if persisted in, will be sure, in time, to wreck the peace and happiness of yourself and family.

Extravagance is, no doubt, often the result of mere thoughtlessness, but that does not mend matters. There is as much evil wrought by want of thought as by want of heart. If it is true that there is but one step between the sublime and the ridiculous, it is equally true that there is but one step between folly and wickedness. Therefore, all young housekeepers ought to give earnest attention to the management of their affairs, for certainly in these matters the 'wise woman buildeth her house, while the foolish plucketh it down with her hands.'

FOOD AND DIET.

The human body is constantly wearing out. With every movement, every breath drawn, there is some waste of its substance. To repair this waste, and, in the case of children, to provide material for their growth, a certain amount of food should be taken daily. The food taken should consist of such qualities as will make flesh and muscle; such as will also keep up the heat of the body, and give force, or the power of movement. These foods must contain a certain quantity of liquid, and the salts necessary to keep the blood pure.

Table of Foods.

Flesh-forming or Nitrogenous.	Heat-giving or Carbonaceous.
Examples—Meat	*Examples*—Butter
Poultry	Suet
Fish	Dripping
Game	And fat of all kinds
Eggs	Sugar in whatever form
Cheese	Starch, which is contained in all vegetables
Flour	
Oatmeal	
Barley	
Rice	
Peas	
Beans	
Lentils	

The foods under the head of flesh-formers, although classed as flesh-formers, are really compound foods. They contain some heat-giving as well as flesh-forming properties.

The heat-giving foods, on the contrary, are all simple foods. Life could not be sustained on any one of them alone, whatever quantity might be taken. These facts are sufficient to show the necessity of a mixed diet. Professor Church says in his lectures on this subject: 'Our food must be palatable, that we may eat it with relish, and get the greatest nourishment from it. The flavour and texture of food, its taste, in fact, stimulates the production of those secretions—such as the saliva and the gastric juice—by the action of which the food is digested or dissolved, and becomes finally a part of the body, or is *assimilated*. As food, then, must be relished it is desirable that it should be varied in character—it should neither be restricted to vegetable products on the one hand, nor to animal substances (including milk and eggs) on the other. By due admixture of these, and by varying, occasionally, the kind of vegetable or meat taken, or the modes of cooking adopted, the necessary constituents of a diet are furnished more cheaply, and at the same time do more efficiently their proper work. Now, if we were to confine ourselves to wheaten bread, we should be obliged to eat in order to obtain our daily supply of albuminoids, or 'flesh-formers,' nearly 4 lb.—an amount that would give us nearly twice as much of the starchy matters which should accompany the albuminoids—or, in other words, it would supply not more than the necessary daily allowance of *nitrogen*, but almost twice the necessary daily allowance of *carbon*. Now animal food is generally richer in albuminoid, or nitrogenous constituents, than vegetable food; so, by mixing lean meat with our bread, we may get a food in which the constituents correspond better to our requirements; for 2 lb. of bread may be substituted by 12 oz. of meat, and yet all the necessary carbon as well as nitrogen be thereby supplied. As such a substitution is often too expensive, owing to the high price of meat—cheese, which is twice as rich in nitrogenous matters (that is flesh-formers) as butchers' meat, may be, and constantly is, employed as a complete diet, and for persons in health, doing hard bodily work, it affords suitable nourishment. Even some vegetable products, rich in nitrogen, as haricot beans, may be used in the same way as meat or cheese, and for the same purpose.'[1]

It is a pity that the value of haricot beans, peas, lentils, and oatmeal is not more generally known. One writer says that there is as much nourishment in 1 lb. of either of these as in 3 lb. of lean meat; and in a lecture on the same subject, another writer states that in three farthings' worth of oatmeal there is as much nourishment as in a mutton chop. These are certainly facts which should be known, especially by people of limited means. Macaroni and semolina are also valuable foods; they are prepared from the most nutritious part of the wheat grain. Rice and maize are deficient in flesh-forming properties, but useful as heat-giving foods; so are, also, tapioca, cornflour, and sago.

Potatoes and fresh vegetables contain but little nourishment. They must not, however, be despised on that account, as they are most valuable additions to our daily diet on account of the potash and other salts which they contain. These vegetables help to keep the blood pure. The anti-scorbutic properties of the potato are so great, that since its introduction into England leprosy is said to have entirely disappeared; neither is scurvy the scourge it was formerly.

The food taken daily should be in proportion to the work done. A labouring man, for example, working hard each day, would require such foods as liver and bacon, steak, bullock's heart, beans, peas, cheese, hard-boiled eggs, &c.; foods, in fact, that would not be too easily digested. Hard work causes the food to be assimilated more readily. A too easily digested fare would cause a constant feeling of hunger. For anyone, on the contrary, leading a sedentary life, the food taken could not be too digestible. In that case, mutton, plainly cooked chicken, soles, milk puddings, and lightly boiled eggs should be the kind of viands chosen.

Children should have plain wholesome fare. Oatmeal and bread are both excellent foods for them. The lime they contain hardens their bones. The bread should be made from seconds flour, which contains more flesh-forming and mineral matter than the whiter and more sifted kinds.

Children should also have plenty of good milk. This is of the greatest importance, especially for the first months of a child's life. Milk is the only perfect food, and contains all that is necessary to sustain healthy life. It is also the only food a child can properly digest, until it cuts its teeth. The improper feeding of children is the great cause of infant mortality. When it becomes advisable to add to milk other foods, they should be nutritious and well cooked. Fine oatmeal or baked flour are, perhaps, the two best. Dr. Fothergill says: 'Children fed on the food of their seniors, or rich cake, and crammed with sweeties, do not as a rule thrive well. They cannot compare favourably with children fed on oatmeal, maize, and milk. Oatmeal is recovering its position as a nursery food, after its temporary banishment. Oatmeal porridge is the food *par excellence* of the infants born north of the Trent, or was, at least, and stalwart people were the results.'

There is no doubt oatmeal is an excellent food, not for children only, but for everyone, especially for those who work hard. It is much to be regretted that it is not more universally used. The English, as a rule, eat too much animal food; and do not give sufficient attention to the proper preparation of vegetables.

Oatmeal water is considered a most strengthening beverage, and is used by men in foundries when beer and fermented liquors would be found too heating.

Of alcoholic drinks, Mr. Buckmaster says (echoing the opinion of eminent physiologists): 'BEER, WINE, and SPIRITS are never to be regarded as foods. Their popular use is entirely due to their stimulating properties. They contain no nitrogen, and are therefore not flesh-formers, nor can they add anything to the wasting tissues. All stimulants act by increasing, for a time, the vitality of the body; but this activity is always followed by depression in proportion to the previous excitement. TEA and COFFEE do, to some extent, prevent waste; but their value as foods depends mainly on the sugar and milk taken with them; and their use, *instead of food*, is almost as hurtful as intoxicating drinks. COCOA differs very much from either tea or coffee, since it is a nutritious liquid food.'

In a lecture on the action of alcohol upon health, Sir Andrew Clark says of health: 'That it is a state which cannot be benefited by alcohol in any degree.' He also states: 'It is capable of proof, beyond all possibility of question, that alcohol, *in ordinary circumstances, not only does not help work, but is a serious hindrance of work.*'

These facts are so important, and ought to be so universally known, that it is to be hoped before long the chemistry of food will occupy the place it should as one of the most necessary branches of everyone's education.

THE TABLE.

> A properly cooked meal, and a neatly arranged dinner-table, are helps to the happiness and moral progress of the humblest of families.—BUCKMASTER.

A REALLY capable housekeeper will not be satisfied with good cookery only. She will be careful to have each dish nicely served, however plain it may be. Culture, or the want of it, will be seen at once in the appointment of her table. This remark does not apply to a profusion of glass, silver, or flowers—these are questions of wealth—but to the neatness and order with which a table is laid, and the manner in which the meal is served.

Some people are particularly sensitive to external impressions; and to them a dinner, or any other meal, however costly, served in an untidy room, with table-cloth soiled, silver tarnished, glasses smeared, and above all a slovenly servant, would be enough to give a feeling of depression that would anything but aid digestion.

A great point to be attended to is to have everything perfectly clean and orderly, however old and plain. Clean table-cloths make a wonderful difference to the look of a table; a few flowers also will do much to give it a bright appearance. Servants should be neat in their dress, and quiet in their movements. If only one is kept, that is no reason why she should wait at table in a slovenly dress and with ruffled hair.

The dining-room should be, if possible, a bright room with a good aspect. Heavy, sombre furniture, however fashionable, should be avoided. It is unfortunate that so little attention is paid to the influence of colour; a warm colouring will do much to give a bright look to a room which would otherwise be dull.

The influence of the mental emotions on the digestion is so great that it is important that the conversation at meals should be as cheerful as possible, and no unpleasant subject should be discussed: anything that disturbs the appetite disturbs the digestion also.

With these points carefully attended to—a bright room, neatly-laid table, well-cooked food, and cheerful conversation—dinner, or any other meal, will become what it should be, a refreshment to both mind and body.

HOW TO COOK.

Hints to Beginners.

A FEW hints to beginners on the proper way to set about their work may be, perhaps, of some use; as I know many people get disgusted with cookery at the very outset, and after one attempt, form a resolution never to enter the kitchen again. They have spent the whole morning trying to make a single dish, and that has proved a failure; they have become hot, tired, and irritable, and ill able to bear the laughter their failure has excited. There has been a waste of material to no purpose, and they conclude, therefore, that it is useless for *them* to make any further attempts. At any rate, they determine that they will not try again 'just yet;' and that often means that they do not try again at all. This disappointment and fatigue is generally the result of want of method and forethought. A recipe has been taken into the kitchen to be tried; very probably one half of the terms used in it have not been understood by the would-be cook. She at once begins to make the dish, going to the recipe to look for each article required as she wants to use it. If some of the supplies have run short, she has perhaps to wait in the middle of her operations while she sends to purchase them. Moreover, when the cake, pastry, or whatever it may be, is made, the fire has very likely been forgotten. In this way, even if the dish has been properly prepared, it is spoiled in the cooking.

Those, too, who have some knowledge of the art and perhaps, can cook fairly well, will often find the work a great fatigue and toil. They spend double or treble the time they need in the kitchen, just for the want of a little judicious management.

Before trying a recipe read it over, *carefully* notice how a dish is to be cooked, and make up the fire accordingly. If it is pastry, take means to get the oven hot; if a boiled pudding, make a good fire, and put a large saucepan of water on to cook it in before doing anything else. When this most important matter is attended to, put all the materials required on the table with the weights and scales; notice what cooking utensils will be required, see that they are all clean and ready for use, and put them near to hand. If, for example, you want to make a cake, proceed in this manner:—Attend first to the fire to get the oven lightly heated, then put out the weights and scales and all necessary materials; put a basin on the table for mixing, two or three cups for breaking eggs in, one or two plates to put the different ingredients on as they are measured, a grater, and anything else that may be required. Then carefully weigh the materials, taking the exact quantities named in the recipe. Prepare them all before mixing any of them. Wash and pick over the currants, and while they are drying, cut up all the candied peel; beat up the eggs, and grease and prepare the cake-tin. The butter should then be rubbed into the flour, and the other dry ingredients should be added. The cake should then be quickly mixed, put into its tin, and placed at once in a hot oven.

If several dishes are to be made, a little thought beforehand will often prevent a very great deal of fatigue and waste of time. Suppose, for example, that you wish to prepare two or three dishes for supper and to make some cakes for tea. You have, perhaps, decided to have a chicken coated with Béchamel sauce, a *gâteau* of apples with whipped cream, a custard pudding, and some rock cakes. Make, the day before, if possible, a list of the articles required for the different dishes, and order what is necessary in good time, so that there may be no delay the next morning. Have the kitchen quite clear from all litters before you begin to work. No one can cook well in a muddle. Then commence operations by making up the fire and putting a saucepan of stock, or water, on to boil for the chicken. Next put the gelatine to soak for the *gâteau*, not forgetting a little in the Béchamel sauce. The longer gelatine soaks, the more quickly it will dissolve. Then slice the apples and put them to stew with the sugar, so that they may be cooking while you are preparing something else. Afterwards truss the chicken; and probably, by the time it is ready, the water or stock in the saucepan will be boiling. Put the chicken into it to simmer gently, noticing the time, so that it may not be over-cooked. Then prepare the ingredients for the rock cakes; mixing them—as they require a quick oven—before the pudding. While they are cooking, prepare the custard; and by the time it is made, the cakes, if the oven is properly hot, will be sufficiently set to admit of the heat being moderated. Now make the Béchamel sauce; strain it and add the dissolved gelatine. Take up the chicken, remove the skewers, place it on a dish, and coat it nicely with the sauce. Then rub the apples through the sieve, and finish making the *gâteau*. By this time the chicken, *gâteau*, and rock cakes are made, and the custard will be cooking. While waiting for the custard, whip the cream for the *gâteau* and put it on a sieve to drain; prepare any decorations you may intend to put on the fowl, and lay them on a plate near to it in the pantry, ready to put on just before serving. Everything will now be ready. With just a little management, even a slow worker would scarcely take a longer time to make these dishes than an hour and a half.

Whatever failures and disappointments you may meet with at first, do not be discouraged. Success is certain if you will only have a little patience and perseverance. Do not be disheartened because you feel very awkward, and because you not unfrequently forget the oven, and let your cakes and pastry burn. Try not to mind the banter of your relations and friends at any possible failure. Many well-meaning efforts to acquire this useful knowledge have been nipped in the bud by the thoughtless, silly way in which some people will laugh at any mistake or blunder. A cake which has caught in baking, or a pudding with the sugar left out, will probably afford them an inexhaustible subject of mirth. Make up your mind, however, not to be discouraged by any of these things. Practice will give nimbleness to your fingers and strength to your memory. As regards any laughter your mistakes may cause, only persevere, and it will not be long before the laugh will be on your side. But keep in mind in any of your attempts that you must be *exact* in all you do. If you try to cook without paying strict attention to weights of the materials to be used and to the other directions, you will deserve to fail. Be very particular in measuring quantities; bear in mind that carelessness in this respect is no mark of a superior cook as some people imagine, but rather of a careless or ignorant one.

As whatever is worth doing at all is worth doing well, bring all your intelligence to bear upon what you take in hand.

HOW TO CLEAN STOVES AND COOKING UTENSILS.

Iron Saucepans.

IMMERSE them in a pan of hot water with soda in it, and wash them thoroughly inside and out, taking care that nothing is left sticking to the bottom of the saucepans. If anything has been burnt in them, boil some strong soda and water in them before washing them, and then rub the bottom of the saucepan with sand until it is quite clean. The sand must be used nearly dry; if too much wetted it loses its power.

The saucepan lids should be thoroughly rinsed and dried.

Enamel Saucepans.

Wash them thoroughly in hot water with soda in it, using soap if necessary. If anything has been burnt in the saucepan, boil strong soda and water in it before cleaning it, and rub it well with sand. Rinse and dry thoroughly.

Anglo-American Saucepans.

Clean like enamel saucepans. They should be kept perfectly clean inside and out.

Tin Saucepans.

Clean these like iron saucepans.

Dish Covers and Jelly Moulds.

Wash with soap and water and dry thoroughly. Powder some whiting, and mix with a little cold water; brush the mixture over the covers and moulds; when dry, rub off with a plate brush or soft cloth or leather.

To Clean a Roaster.

Wash the dripping-pan and inside of the roaster with hot water and soda to remove all grease, then rub them with sand until they are quite bright, rinse and dry thoroughly. Clean the outside of the roaster with whiting, used according to directions given for cleaning dish covers.

Hair and Wire Sieves.

Wash these thoroughly with hot water with soda in it, and scrub them quite clean with a sieve-brush. Dry them thoroughly, and keep them in a *dry place*. If this is not done a hair sieve will get mildewed, an iron one rusty, and a copper one will verdigris and become poisonous. Copper-wire sieves should always have especial care.

Paste Boards and Rolling Pins.

Scrub them well with hot water and sand. Do not use soda, as it will make the wood yellow.

Baking Tins.

Wash them in hot water with soda in it, and rub with sand until they are bright; rinse and dry well.

To Clean a Close Stove or Open Range.

Scrape out all the ashes and brush up all the dust. Then, with a brush, thoroughly clean the flues. Brush the stove over with liquid blacklead, and when it is dry polish with brushes. Then clean any steel about the stove and the fire-irons and fender with emery-paper; any brass with brick-dust well rubbed on with a leather.

Brush all the dust from the oven, and wipe it round with a cloth wrung out of hot water.

To Clean a Gas Stove.

Wash off any grease that may have been spilled on the stove with a cloth dipped in hot water, and wipe the inside of the stove, taking care to dry it thoroughly. Wash the dripping-pan in hot water with soda in it, and rub it with sand to brighten it. Then wipe it quite dry.

Brush the stove over with liquid blacklead, and polish it with brushes.

Copper Cooking Utensils.

Wash them well in hot water with soda in it; moisten some salt with vinegar, and rub them well with this to remove stains and tarnish. Then wash them quickly with soap and water, and dry them thoroughly; polish them with a little powdered whiting rubbed on with a soft leather.

RULES FOR BOILING.

ALL meat, with the exception of salt meat, should be put into boiling water, and should be well boiled for quite five minutes, in order that the albumen on the outside of the joint may be set. The hardened albumen forms a kind of casing. This casing serves to keep in, as far as possible, the flavour and juices of the meat. When the meat has been boiled sufficiently long to effect this hardening, the kettle should be drawn to one side of the fire. The water should be kept at simmering point until the joint is cooked. The general rule, as regards time required for boiling, is a quarter of an hour for each pound of meat and a quarter of an hour over. But only general rules can be given, as the time will vary according to the nature of the joint to be cooked. A thick piece of meat will necessarily take longer to cook than a thin piece with much bone, although both may be the same weight. Very *fresh* meat will also take longer to cook than that which has been hung.

As soon as the water boils, after the meat is in it, the scum should be carefully removed from time to time, while it is cooking. If the scum be allowed to boil down, it will settle on the joint and discolour it. It is best, however, as a precaution, to wrap the meat in a very clean cloth; this will effectually preserve its colour. Salt meat should be put into lukewarm water, for the purpose of drawing out some of the salt. It should be simmered gently, allowing always twenty minutes to the pound, and twenty minutes over. Salt hardens the fibre of the meat; it, therefore, requires to be cooked for a longer time to make it tender.

RULES FOR ROASTING.

To roast successfully, make up a nice clear fire. When once made up, it should be replenished, if necessary, by putting on coal or coke at the back. The live coals should be drawn to the front to prevent smoke. Fasten the joint to the jack. Place the roaster close to the fire for the first ten minutes, so that the heat of the fire may at once harden the albumen, and form a case to keep in the flavour and juices. Afterwards, draw the roaster farther back and cook gradually, basting every ten minutes. The basting keeps the meat from drying up, and gives it a better flavour. The length of time allowed for roasting is the same as for boiling, the rule being a quarter of an hour for each pound, and a quarter of an hour over. For white meat, veal and pork, or solid joints without bone, allow twenty minutes to the pound, and twenty minutes over. These rules, however, cannot always be strictly adhered to, as the size and shape of the joint must be taken into consideration, as well as the weight. Meat that has been frozen will take longer to cook than fresh meat. Meat which has been well hung will take a shorter time than fresh meat. If a jack is not used, the joint should be fastened to a rope of worsted, which should be kept constantly turning.

Gravy, for a joint, may be made according to two methods. The first method is to take the dripping-pan away half an hour before the joint is cooked, then to put a hot dish in its place, and to pour the contents of the pan into a basin. Put the basin into a refrigerator; or, place it on ice. As soon as it is cold, the fat will cake on the top of the gravy, and should be removed very carefully. Make the gravy hot, diluting it with warm water, if necessary, and pour it round the joint.

The other and more usual method of making gravy, is to pour away all the fat from the pan as soon as the joint is cooked; and then pour into the pan a sufficient quantity of hot water, scraping well the brown glaze from the bottom; colour carefully with caramel, or burnt sugar, and pour it *round* the joint, not *over* it. Pouring the gravy over the meat destroys its crispness.

On no account make gravy from stock; stock is quite unsuitable, as the vegetable flavour is, to many persons, disagreeable.

RULES FOR FRYING.

French or Wet Frying.

THIS is cooking in a large quantity of fat sufficient to cover the articles fried in it. Oil, lard, dripping, or fat rendered down, may be used for this purpose. Oil is considered the best, as it will rise to 600° without burning; other fats get over-heated after 400°, and therefore require greater care in using. Success depends, almost entirely, on getting the fat to the right degree of heat. For ordinary frying, the heat required is 345°. Unless this point is carefully attended to, total failure will be the result. There are signs, however, by which anyone may easily tell when the fat is ready for use. It must be quite still, making no noise; noise, or bubbling, will be caused by the evaporation of moisture, or water in it. The expression, 'boiling lard,' or 'boiling fat,' has been misleading to many inexperienced cooks, who, not unnaturally, imagine that when the fat is bubbling, like boiling water, it is boiling, and, therefore, at the right heat. But boiling *fat* does not bubble. When it has the appearance of boiling water, it is simply due, as already explained, to the presence of water in it, which must pass away by evaporation, before the fat can reach the required heat. When it ceases to make any noise, and is quite still, it should be carefully watched; for very soon a pale blue vapour is seen rising, and then the fat is sufficiently hot. If, from the position of the stove, it is not easy to see this vapour, a piece of bread may be held in the fat as a test; if it begins to turn brown, in about a minute, the fat is ready. It should then be used without delay; since, when once hot enough, it rapidly gets overheated or burnt. Fat is burning when the blue vapour becomes like smoke. Burnt fat has an unpleasant smell, and is apt to give a disagreeable taste to the articles fried in it. With ordinary care fat need not get overheated. Next to oil, fat rendered down (*see* Rendering down Fat), is best for the purpose. If strained after each time of using, and not allowed to burn, it will keep good for months, and may be used for fish, sweets, or savouries, and no taste of anything previously fried in it will be given to the articles cooked. For this kind of frying, a kitchener, or gas stove, is preferable to an open range.

All kinds of rissoles, croquettes, fillets and cutlets of fish, fritters, &c., should be fried in this manner, and should not be darker than a golden brown. It is an advantage to use a frying-basket for all such things as are covered with egg and bread-crumbs; but fritters, or whatever is dipped in batter, should be dropped into the fat, as they become so light that they rise to the top of it. When they are a pale fawn colour on the one side, they should be turned over to the other. Care must be taken to drain everything, after frying, on kitchen paper in order to remove any grease.

Dry Frying.

This is frying in a cutlet or frying pan, with a small quantity of fat, and is only suitable for such things as require slow cooking, such as steaks, mutton or veal cutlets, fillets of beef, liver and bacon. Pancakes also are fried in this manner. Success depends, as in French frying, in having the fat rightly heated, taking care that the outside of the meat cooked be sealed up. In this way the juices and flavour will be retained in it. Make, therefore, the frying-pan hot, then put in the fat; and when that is also perfectly hot, put in the meat to be cooked. When each side has been well sealed up, the heat applied must be moderated, so that the cooking may be gradual. The common mistake in this kind of frying is to put the meat into the fat when it is but barely melted; the juices of the meat are thus allowed to escape, and the meat is toughened.

RULES FOR BAKING.

To bake meat successfully, the oven must be well ventilated, otherwise, the joint cooked in this manner will have an unpleasant flavour. The meat should be put on a trivet, which should be placed on a baking-tin. The oven must be very hot when the meat is put into it, and the heat should be kept up for the first quarter of an hour. This is to form the casing already alluded to in the directions for roasting and boiling; the heat of the oven must then be very much moderated, and the joint cooked very gradually, allowing twenty minutes for every pound, and twenty minutes over. The meat should be basted; and the gravy may be made in the same manner as in roasting.

JOINTS.

Sirloin of Beef.

This is the primest joint, and must be either roasted or baked (see directions). Horse-radish should be served with it. Yorkshire pudding is also liked with roast beef.

Ribs of Beef.

These should be cooked like sirloin, and served with the same accompaniments. A neater looking joint is made by boning and rolling them. The bones can be used for soup.

Aitch Bone, Round, Thick and Thin Flank of Beef.

Those are usually salted and boiled (see directions for boiling salt meat). Serve with carrots and turnips, and yeast, Norfolk, or suet dumplings.

Brisket of Beef.

This should be stewed (see directions for stewed brisket).

Leg of Mutton.

This may be roasted, baked, or boiled. If roasted, it should be served with red-currant jelly; if boiled, with caper sauce. Carrots and turnips are liked with boiled mutton.

Shoulder of Mutton.

This may be either roasted or baked. Serve with onion sauce.

Saddle of Mutton.

This may be either roasted or baked. Serve with red-currant jelly.

Neck of Mutton.

This is boiled, and requires long and gentle cooking. Serve with caper sauce.

Fore Quarter of Lamb.

This joint should be roasted or baked. Serve with mint sauce.

Leg of Lamb.

This may be either roasted, baked, or boiled. Serve, if roast, with mint sauce; and if boiled, with *maître d'hôtel* sauce.

Shoulder of Lamb, Saddle of Lamb, Loin of Lamb

All these are either roasted or boiled, and served with mint sauce.

Fillet of Veal.

Stuff it with veal stuffing and make into nice round shape; fasten it securely with string and skewers, and roast or bake it. Serve with cut lemon, and send some boiled ham, pork, or bacon to table with it. Use a pint of thin melted butter, instead of water, for making the gravy.

Breast, Shoulder, and Loin of Veal.

These are all roasted. Thin melted butter is used to make the gravy for them, and cut lemon is served with them.

Knuckle of Veal.

This is boiled, and served with one dessertspoonful of chopped parsley added to one pint of melted butter.

Leg of Pork.

This must be roasted or baked, the skin having been previously scored with a knife. Serve it with apple sauce.

Chine of Pork.

Stuff it with pork stuffing (see Forcemeats) and roast it. Serve with apple sauce.

Spare Rib of Pork.

This is roasted, the skin having previously been scored. Serve it with apple sauce.

Hand of Pork.

Soak it for two or three hours before cooking, and boil it. Serve with pease pudding.

Leg of Pork.

This joint is also salted and boiled. It is served with pease pudding.

To Cook a Ham.

Put into lukewarm water, to which has been added one pint of old ale. Simmer it very gently until quite tender. For a ham always allow twenty-five minutes to each pound, and twenty-five minutes over. Let it get cold in the liquor in which it boiled, then remove the rind and carefully cover with raspings.

Bacon.

Cook like ham, taking care that it is simmered until perfectly tender. Remove the skin and cover with raspings.

Pickled Pork.

Put it into lukewarm water and simmer gently until tender.

POULTRY AND GAME.

Roast Goose.

Ingredients—1 Goose.

Sage and onion stuffing.

1½ oz. of flour.

1 onion.

1 apple.

3 sage leaves.

½ lb. of gravy beef.

1 quart of water.

Method.—Stuff the goose by placing the sage and onion forcemeat inside it.

Then truss it nicely and roast it from one and a half to two hours.

If it is a large one, two hours; if a small one, one and a half hours.

To make the gravy, simmer the giblets in water for three hours with half a pound of gravy beef cut in pieces, a sliced onion, apple, and three sage leaves, pepper and salt.

Then stir in a thickening made of the flour, and colour the gravy with a little burnt sugar. If liked, a glass of port wine may be added.

Pour a little gravy round the goose, and serve the rest in a tureen.

Apple or tomato sauce should be served with roast goose.

Roast Turkey.

Ingredients—1 turkey.

Some veal forcemeat (omitting the suet).

1 lb. of gravy beef.

3 pints of water.

1 onion.

2 oz. of flour.

Method.—Place the forcemeat inside the turkey, and truss it nicely.

Roast it from one and a half to two and a half hours.

Make the gravy by simmering the giblets and beef in the water with the onion for three hours.

Thicken the gravy with the flour, and pour a little round the turkey.

Serve the rest in a tureen.

Place some fried or baked sausages round the turkey, and serve with bread sauce.

Boiled Turkey.

A small turkey is sometimes boiled like a fowl, and served with oyster, celery, or Béchamel sauce.

Roast Duck.

Ingredients—1 duck.

Some sage and onion stuffing.

Rather more than 1 pint water.

1 oz. of flour.

1 onion.

1 apple.

¼ lb. of gravy beef, or 2 or 3 bones.

Method.—Stuff the duck by placing the forcemeat inside it.

Truss it nicely, and roast it from three-quarters of an hour to an hour, according to its size.

Make the gravy by simmering the giblets in the water with the beef or bones, onion, apple, pepper and salt, for two hours.

Thicken it with the flour, and colour carefully with burnt sugar.

Pour a little gravy round the duck, and serve the rest in a tureen.

A glass of port wine may be added to the gravy if liked.

Apple or tomato sauce should be served with roast duck.

Ducklings.

These are cooked and served like ducks, and take from twenty to forty minutes to roast, according to their size.

Roast Hare.

Ingredients—1 hare.

Some veal forcemeat.

½ lb. of gravy beef.

1 pint of water.

1 onion.

1 oz. of flour.

Pepper and salt.

Method.—Stuff the belly of the hare with the forcemeat, and sew it in.

Truss it nicely, and roast it from one and a quarter to two hours, according to its size, basting it constantly.

To make gravy, cut the beef into small pieces, and simmer in the water, with the onion sliced, for three hours. Thicken it with the flour, and add, if liked, a glass of port wine.

Pour a little gravy round the hare, and serve the remainder in a tureen.

Jugged Hare.

Ingredients—1 hare.
Some veal forcemeat.
2 oz. of butter.
1 onion, stuck with 6 cloves.
2 glasses of port wine.
1½ pint of gravy or stock.
1 lemon.

Method.—Dry the hare well and cut it in pieces.

Fry them in the butter.

Then remove them and fry the flour a nice brown.

Pour in the gravy or stock, and stir until it boils.

Then put the stock into an earthenware jar with the hare, onion, thin rind and juice of the lemon, and pepper and salt to taste.

Cover the jar close, and put it into a moderate oven, where it must simmer gently from three to four hours until the hare is quite tender.

Make some balls of veal forcemeat, to which the chopped liver of the hare has been added, and either fry or bake them.

Add them to the jugged hare, and, last of all, pour in the wine.

Serve with red-currant jelly.

Roast Rabbit.

Ingredients—1 rabbit.
Some veal forcemeat.
Some nice gravy (*see* Gravy).

Method.—Fill the belly of the rabbit with the forcemeat, and sew it in.

Truss it nicely, and roast it from three-quarters to one hour, basting constantly.

Pour a little gravy round it, and send some to table in a tureen.

Serve with red-currant jelly.

Boiled Rabbit.

Ingredients—1 rabbit.

Some onion or *maître d'hôtel* sauce.

Method.—Boil the rabbit gently from half an hour to an hour, according to its size and age.

Serve it with onion or *maître d'hôtel* sauce.

Stewed Rabbits.

Ingredients—2 rabbits.

4 large onions.

3 pints of water.

2½ oz. of flour.

Pepper and salt to taste.

Method.—Cut the rabbits into joints, and slice the onions.

Put them with the water into a large stewpan, and simmer for one hour or more until the rabbits are tender.

Then make a thickening of the flour and stir it in, letting it boil well.

Put the rabbit on a hot dish, and pour the gravy over.

Ragout of Rabbit.

Ingredients—1 rabbit.

1 onion stuck with 6 cloves.

2 oz. of butter or dripping.

1 oz. of flour.

1½ pint of water or stock.

Pepper and salt to taste.

Method.—Cut the rabbit into neat joints, and fry them in a stewpan in the butter or dripping.

When brown remove them and fry the flour.

Then pour in the water or stock, and stir until it boils.

Put in the pieces of rabbit with the onion, and pepper and salt to taste.

Simmer gently for about one hour or more until quite tender.

Serve the rabbit on a hot dish, and strain the gravy over it.

Roast Pheasant.

Ingredients—1 pheasant.

Half a pint of gravy.

Butter.

Method.—Roast the pheasant nicely for three-quarters of an hour or an hour, according to its size, basting it constantly with butter.

Make a nice gravy for it (*see* Gravy), and serve it with bread sauce and browned crumbs.

Wild Duck.

Ingredients—Wild duck.

Half a pint of gravy (*see* Gravy).

Lemon juice.

Butter.

Method.—Roast the wild duck nicely before a clear fire for thirty or forty-five minutes, basting it constantly with butter.

Sprinkle over it a little cayenne and salt, and a few drops of lemon juice.

Serve the gravy in a tureen.

If liked, a glass of port wine may be poured over the duck.

Partridges.

Partridges should be nicely roasted before a clear fire from twenty-five to thirty minutes.

Serve with a little gravy and bread sauce.

Browned crumbs are also handed with them.

Grouse.

Roast these birds before a nice clear fire, basting constantly with butter.

Serve with gravy, bread sauce, and browned crumbs.

Woodcocks and Snipes.

These birds should be nicely trussed but not drawn.

Roast them carefully from twenty to thirty minutes, basting constantly.

Place under them rounds of toasted bread, buttered on each side, to catch the trail as it drops, as this is considered a delicacy.

When cooked, lay the toast on a hot dish, place the birds on it, and pour a little good gravy over.

Boiled Fowl.

Truss nicely and flour the breast slightly.

Fold it in buttered paper, and tie securely with string.

Boil in stock or water, according to the directions given for boiling meat for three-quarters of an hour to one hour and a half, according to its age and size.

Serve with white, egg, or *maître d'hôtel* sauce poured over it.

Roast Fowl.

Truss nicely and roast, according to directions given for roasting meat, for three-quarters of an hour to one hour and a half according to its age and size.

Serve with bread sauce and some gravy (*see* Gravy).

Braised Partridges.

Ingredients—A brace of partridges.

A small piece of carrot, turnip, and onion.

2 tomatoes.

1 pint of good second stock.

1 wineglass of sherry.

Pepper and salt to taste.

Method.—Truss two partridges as for boiling.

Put at the bottom of a stewpan the vegetables cut in small pieces.

Lay the partridges on the top and pour in the stock and sherry; these should be sufficient to come half way up the partridges.

Cover with buttered paper.

Put the lid on the stewpan and simmer very gently until the partridges are tender.

Then put them on a baking tin in the oven to brown them.

Strain the stock and boil it rapidly down to a glaze.

Serve the partridges with the glaze poured over them.

SAVOURY MEAT DISHES.

Stewed Steak.

Ingredients—1½ lb. of steak.

1 piece of carrot, turnip, onion, and celery.

1 pint of water.

1 oz. of dripping.

1 oz. of flour.

Pepper and salt.

Method.—Cut all the fat from the steak.

Make the dripping hot in a stewpan and fry the steak in it.

Then put in the vegetables, and pour in the water, adding pepper and salt.

Simmer the steak gently from three to four hours, until quite tender.

When quite cooked, remove it from the gravy.

Put it on a hot dish.

Make a thickening of the flour; stir it into the gravy; boil for two minutes, and strain over the steak.

A little mushroom catsup, Harvey, or Worcester sauce may be added if liked.

The fat should previously have been cut into dice, placed on a baking tin, and cooked in the oven.

For serving, put them in the middle of the steak.

Stewed Brisket of Beef.

Ingredients—5 lb. of beef.

2 carrots.

2 onions.

2 turnips.

1 head of celery.

1 sprig of parsley.

Marjoram and thyme.

2 bay leaves.

6 cloves.

1 dozen peppercorns.

3 quarts of water.

Method.—Put the meat into a saucepan with the vegetables and other ingredients, and simmer gently for three hours.

Serve on a hot dish, with some of the liquor for gravy.

The remainder can be made into soup.

If to be eaten cold, remove the bones, and press the beef.

Strain the meat liquor, remove the fat, and boil it down to a glaze.

Brush the meat over with it, giving it as many coats of glaze as necessary.

Stewed Ox-cheek.

Ingredients—1 ox-cheek.

1 cowheel.

3 or 4 carrots.

2 or 3 turnips.

3 or 4 onions.

1 sprig of parsley, thyme, and marjoram.

2 bay leaves.

2 quarts of water.

4 oz. of flour.

Method.—Wash the ox-cheek and cowheel, and cut them into neat pieces.

Put them into the water with the carrots, turnips, and onions, and celery cut in pieces, and the herbs, pepper and salt.

Stew very gently from four to five hours, until the stew is quite tender.

Make a thickening of the flour.

Stir and cook it well in the gravy.

Put the cheek and cowheel on a hot dish, and strain the gravy over them.

The bones can be used for soup.

Mock Hare.

Ingredients—4 lb. shin of beef.

2 quarts of water.

2 carrots.

2 turnips.

1 onion.

6 cloves.

1 sprig of parsley, thyme, and marjoram.

1 glass of port wine.

3 oz. of flour.

Pepper and salt.

Method.—Put the beef into the water with the vegetables cut in pieces, herbs, cloves, pepper and salt, and stew gently from four to five hours, until quite tender.

Then make a thickening of the flour, stir it in, and boil well for two or three minutes.

For serving, place the beef on a hot dish.

Add the wine to the gravy, and strain it over the meat.

Haricot Mutton.

Ingredients—7 or 8 mutton cutlets.

1 pint of second stock.

1 carrot.

1 turnip.

1 onion.

1 stick of celery.

1 oz. of flour.

Pepper and salt.

2 oz. of dripping.

Method.—Fry the cutlets a nice brown in the dripping.

Mix the flour smoothly with the stock; boil it in a stewpan for two minutes.

Then put in the cutlets and the vegetables cut in fancy shapes.

Stew gently for about three-quarters of an hour, until the meat and vegetables are tender.

Dish the cutlets in a circle; place the vegetables round them and pour the gravy over.

Sheep's Head.

Ingredients—1 sheep's head.

1 oz. of butter or dripping.

Pepper and salt.

1½ oz. of flour.

A few drops of lemon juice.

Method.—See that the head has been properly prepared by the butcher, and the nostrils removed.

Soak it well in salt and water, and wash it carefully.

Cut out the tongue, remove the brains, and tie the head into shape with a piece of string.

Put it and the tongue into a saucepan of boiling water, and simmer it from three to four hours.

A quarter of an hour before it is cooked, put in the brains tied in muslin.

To make a sauce for it, melt the butter or dripping in a small stewpan.

Mix in the flour smoothly.

Pour in one pint of the broth from the sheep's head.

Stir and cook well, adding pepper and salt to taste a few drops of lemon juice, or one teaspoonful of vinegar.

Lastly, add the brains, chopped small.

For serving, put the head on a hot dish.

Remove the string, and pour the sauce over.

Sheep's Head au gratin.

Ingredients—1 sheep's head.

2 tablespoonfuls of bread crumbs.

½ oz. of butter.

1 teaspoonful of chopped parsley.

1 teaspoonful of dried and powdered herbs.

Lemon juice.

Pepper and salt.

Method.—Boil the sheep's head according to the directions in preceding recipe.

When cooked, lay it on a greased baking-sheet.

Sprinkle over it the crumbs, parsley, and herbs, adding a few drops of lemon juice; pepper and salt.

Put the butter in little pieces about the head, and brown it in a quick oven or before the fire.

Serve with the brain sauce given in the foregoing recipe.

Liver and Bacon.

Ingredients—1 sheep's liver.

1 lb. of fat bacon.

1 pint of hot water.

Some flour.

Pepper and salt.

Method.—Cut the bacon into slices, and remove the rind.

Cut the liver into slices, and dip them in flour.

Fry the bacon in a frying-pan, then remove it, and fry the liver in the bacon fat, adding a little dripping, if necessary.

When the liver is cooked, place it on a hot dish; dredge the pan with about half an ounce of flour.

Fry the flour brown.

Then pour in one pint of boiling water, stir and boil for one or two minutes; adding pepper and salt to taste.

Place the liver in a circle in the middle of a hot dish.

Put the bacon round it, and strain the gravy over it.

Pigs' Fry, or Mock Goose.

Ingredients—1½ lb. of pigs' fry.

3 lb. of potatoes.

1 onion.

1 apple.

A little sage.

Pepper and salt.

Method.—Boil the potatoes until half-cooked.

Then cut them in slices.

Cut the fry in small pieces.

Chop the onion and apple small.

Dry and powder the sage leaves.

Grease a pie-dish, and put a layer of sliced potatoes at the bottom.

Place on them a layer of pigs' fry.

Sprinkle it with some of the onion, apple, and powdered sage, pepper, and salt.

Cover with another layer of potatoes; and put on that some more of the fry.

Sprinkle again with the onion, apple, pepper, and salt.

Proceed in this way until the dish is full, letting the last layer be potatoes.

Pour in half a pint of water; and cover the dish with a piece of pig's caul, or paper spread with dripping.

Bake in a moderate oven for one hour and a half.

It may be served in the pie-dish, or on a hot dish.

Mock Goose another way.

Ingredients—1½ lb. of pigs' fry.

Some dried and powdered sage.

Chopped apple and onion.

¾ pint of cider.

Pepper and salt.

Method.—Cut the fry in slices.

Thread the pieces on a long skewer.

Lay it on a greased baking-tin, and sprinkle with the onion, apple, sage, pepper, and salt, and cover with the caul.

Bake in a moderate oven until tender.

Then place the fry on a hot dish, and remove the skewer.

Make the cider boiling, and pour over the fry.

Tripe and Onions.

Ingredients—2 lb. of tripe.

3 good-sized onions.

2½ pints of milk.

2 oz. of flour.

Pepper and salt.

Method.—Put the tripe into cold water, and bring it to the boil; this is to blanch it.

Blanch the onions likewise, then throw the water away, and cut the tripe into neat pieces.

Put them in the milk, with the onions cut in halves, and pepper and salt.

Stew gently for an hour.

Then take out the onions and chop them.

Remove the tripe, and put it on a hot dish.

Make a thickening of flour, and boil it well in the milk, and add the chopped onions.

Dish the tripe in a circle, and pour the milk and onions over.

Tripe may be cooked more economically by substituting water for milk.

Stewed Tripe.

Ingredients—2 lb. of tripe.

1 quart of brown sauce (*see* Sauces).

Method.—Blanch the tripe, as in the preceding recipe.

Simmer gently in brown sauce for two hours.

Dish in a circle, with the brown sauce poured over.

Broiled Steak.

Make the gridiron hot, and rub it with fat.

Lay the steak on it.

Place the gridiron close to a clear fire for about two minutes until the heat has scaled up that side of the steak.

Then turn it on to the other side, and let that remain close to the fire for the same length of time.

Then remove it further from the fire and cook more gradually, turning occasionally. It takes from ten to fifteen minutes to cook, according to the thickness of the steak.

Broiled Chop.

Cook like a steak. It will take from seven to ten minutes to cook. Serve very hot.

Fried Steak.

Make the frying-pan quite hot.

Put a little butter or fat in it, and make that quite hot also.

Put in the steak, and fry it over a quick fire for two minutes on one side, then turn it on to the other.

Moderate the heat applied, and cook gently for about twenty minutes, turning occasionally.

Savoury Roast.

Ingredients—1½ lb. of rump or beefsteak, cut thin.

Some veal, or sage-and-onion, stuffing.

¾ oz. of flour.

1 cup of boiling water.

Method.—Lay the stuffing on the steak, roll it round it, and tie it with twine.

Place it in a pie-dish.

Pour the boiling water over it, and place another pie-dish, inverted, at the top of it.

Put it in a moderate oven for two or three hours, until the steak is tender.

Then put the steak on a hot dish.

Thicken the gravy with the flour and pour it over.

Breast of veal may be boned, and stuffed with veal stuffing and cooked in the same way.

Shoulder of Mutton Boned, Stuffed, and Rolled.

Ingredients—1 shoulder of mutton.

Some veal stuffing, or sausage meat.

Method.—Remove the bone carefully, and place some stuffing in the place of it.

Roll up the mutton, and tie it firmly with twine.

It may be roasted, baked, or braised.

If braised, prepare it according to the directions given for braised breast of veal, using a large kettle, if a braising pan is not obtainable.

Braised Breast of Veal.

Ingredients—3 or 4 lb. of breast of veal.

Some veal stuffing.

Some good second stock.

Carrot, turnip, onion.

Sprig of parsley, thyme, marjoram.

1 bay leaf.

Method.—Remove the bones from the veal, and put the stuffing in it.

Roll the veal round it, and sew it or tie it securely with twine.

Put the vegetables, cut in small pieces, in the bottom of a stewpan.

Place the veal on them, and pour in sufficient stock to come half-way up it.

Put the lid on the stewpan, simmer gently until the veal is quite tender, allowing half an hour to each pound and half an hour over.

Then put the veal on a baking-sheet, and put in a quick oven to brown.

Strain the stock into a large stewpan, and boil it rapidly down to a glaze.

Put the veal on a hot dish, remove the string, and pour the glaze over it.

Place round the veal some carrot and turnip, cut in fancy shapes and cooked separately.

Toad-in-the-Hole.

Ingredients—8 oz. of flour.

2 eggs.

1 pint of milk.

1½ lb. of ox kidney.

A little salt.

Method.—Put the flour into a basin.

Make a well in the middle.

Put in the eggs; mix gradually.

Add the milk by degrees.

Beat well, and add the salt.

Cut the kidney in pieces, lay them in a well-greased Yorkshire-pudding tin; and pour the batter over.

Bake from one and a quarter to one and a half hours.

Irish Stew.

Ingredients—2 lb. of potatoes.

1 lb. of scrag end of mutton.

½ lb. of onions.

Pepper and salt.

Method.—Peel and slice the potatoes and onions, and cut the meat into small pieces.

Put a layer of meat in the bottom of a saucepan, then a layer of potatoes, then one of onions.

Season with pepper and salt, and continue placing the ingredients in the saucepan in alternate layers.

Pour in half a pint of water and stew gently, stirring occasionally, for about one hour and a half.

Sea Pie.

Ingredients—2 lb. of steak.

2 onions.

1 carrot.

1 small turnip.

¾ lb. of flour.

¼ lb. of suet.

1 teaspoonful of baking powder.

Pepper and salt to taste.

Cold water.

Method.—Cut the vegetables and meat small, season them with pepper and salt, and put them into a large saucepan.

Put it by the side of the fire for the contents to simmer gently.

Chop the suet finely, add it to the flour and baking powder, and mix with cold water to a stiff paste. Roll it to the size of the saucepan.

Place it over the meat, and simmer gently for two hours.

For serving, remove the crust with a fish slice, put the meat and vegetables on to a hot dish, and place the crust on them.

Roast Bullock's Heart.

Ingredients—1 bullock's heart.

Some veal stuffing (double the quantity given in the recipe).

Method.—Wash the heart in salt and water, and cleanse it thoroughly.

Wipe it quite dry.

Cut off the flaps and fill the cavities with the stuffing.

Grease a piece of paper with dripping, and tie it firmly over the top of the heart to keep in the forcemeat.

Roast it according to the directions for roasting meat; it will take about two hours.

Gravy for the Heart.

Ingredients—1 pint of stock.

The trimmings from the heart.

1 onion.

1 oz. of butter.

1 oz. of flour.

A little Harvey's sauce or catsup.

A little burnt sugar, if necessary, for colouring.

Method.—Put the trimmings into a saucepan with the onion and water, and simmer gently while the heart is cooking.

Then melt the butter in a stewpan.

Mix in the flour smoothly; add the liquor strained.

Stir and boil three minutes; add the sauce, pepper and salt, and colouring.

Put the heart on a hot dish, remove the paper, and pour the gravy round it.

If preferred, the heart may be baked.

SAUCES.

SAUCES are often failures, chiefly because they are not made of a proper consistency; and because the flour in them is not sufficiently cooked. It should be remembered that the starch in flour wants to be *well boiled*, otherwise it will be indigestible, and the sauce will have a raw, pasty taste. A sauce is not ready when it *thickens*, but should be boiled for quite three minutes. Its consistency should depend on what it is to be used for. Ordinary sauces, served in a sauce tureen, should be fairly thick; the proportions taken should be 1 oz. of butter; ¾ oz. of flour; ½ pint of milk. If the sauce is to be used to coat anything very thinly (new potatoes, for example), ½ oz. of flour, instead of ¾ oz., would be sufficient. If a sauce is required to entirely mask a small piece of fish, or chicken, &c., 1 oz. of flour should be used, with the proportions of milk and butter already given. Every ingredient should be properly weighed or measured. Carelessness in this respect is a mark of ignorance, and *must* occasion failures.

For making most of the ordinary sauces, the butter is melted first in a small stewpan, care being taken that it does not discolour; the flour is then mixed with it. If the mixing is not perfect, the sauce will be lumpy. The milk, stock, or water, is then poured in, and the sauce is stirred *one way*, until it has boiled three minutes. If cream is used, it is then added, and allowed just to boil in the sauce.

In making economical sauces, when less butter and flour are used (*see* Economical Family Sauce), the method employed is different. The flour is then mixed very smoothly with a little of the milk, water, or whatever is used, and then added to the remainder, which may be cold or boiling; but greater care is required to keep it smooth when the liquid is poured in boiling.

English Melted Butter.

Ingredients—1 oz. of butter.

¾ oz. of flour.

½ pint of water.

Pepper and salt.

Method.—Melt the butter in a small stewpan.

Mix in the flour smoothly.

Add the water; stir and cook well.

Then add pepper and salt, and it is ready to serve.

Plain White Sauce.

Ingredients—1 oz. of butter.

¾ oz. of flour.

½ pint of milk.

A few drops of lemon juice.

Pepper and salt.

Method.—Melt the butter in a small stewpan.

Mix in the flour smoothly.

Add the milk.

Stir and cook well.

Then add the lemon juice and seasoning.

A little cream may also be added if desired.

Maître d'Hôtel Sauce.

Ingredients—¾ oz. of butter.

½ oz. of flour.

½ pint of milk.

A few drops of lemon juice.

Pepper and salt.

A teaspoonful of finely-chopped parsley.

Method.—Melt the butter in a small stewpan.

Mix in the flour smoothly.

Add the milk; stir and cook well.

Then add the lemon juice, seasoning, and chopped parsley.

Mayonnaise Sauce.

Ingredients—2 yolks of eggs.

1 gill of salad oil.

2 tablespoonfuls of taragon vinegar.

Pepper and salt.

Method.—Put the yolks, which must be perfectly free from the whites, into a basin, which in summer time should be placed on ice.

Work them well with a whisk or wooden spoon, adding the oil drop by drop.

When the sauce is so thick that the whisk, or spoon, is moved with difficulty, the oil may be added more quickly, but still very gradually.

Lastly, add the taragon vinegar and seasoning.

Note.—Success in making this sauce depends on first dividing the yolks completely from the whites. Secondly, in keeping them and the oil quite cold. Thirdly, on adding the oil, drop by drop, until the sauce is perfectly thick. If the sauce is made in a warm place, or the oil mixed in too quickly, it is apt to curdle. Should this occur, put a yolk in another basin and very slowly add the sauce to it, stirring briskly; this will generally make it smooth again. Two yolks will be sufficient for any quantity of sauce, taragon vinegar being added in proportion to the oil used.

Tartare Sauce.

Ingredients—2 yolks.

¼ pint of salad oil.

2 tablespoonfuls of taragon vinegar.

1 teaspoonful of finely-chopped parsley.

A few capers, or a chopped gherkin.

Pepper and salt.

If liked, a teaspoonful of ready-made mustard.

Method.—Proceed as in making Mayonnaise Sauce; adding when the sauce is ready the parsley, capers, mustard, and seasoning.

Egg Sauce.

Ingredients—1 oz. of butter.

¾ oz. of flour.

½ pint of milk.

Lemon juice.

Pepper and salt.

1 or 2 hard-boiled eggs.

Method.—Melt the butter in a small stewpan.

Mix in the flour smoothly.

Add the milk, and stir and cook well.

Then add the lemon juice, seasoning, and the chopped whites of the eggs.

If a very thick sauce is required, take 1 oz. of flour. Cream may be added if desired.

Brown Sauce.

Ingredients—2 oz. of butter.

1½ oz. of flour.

A small piece of carrot, turnip, and onion.

A few button mushrooms.

1 pint of good stock.

A few drops of lemon juice.

Seasoning to taste.

Method.—Put the butter into a stewpan and fry the vegetables in it.
Then mix in the flour and fry that.
Add the stock; stir and cook well.
Squeeze in the lemon juice, and add the seasoning.
Strain through a tammy-cloth or fine strainer.

Genoise Sauce.

Ingredients—1 oz. of butter.

¾ oz. of flour.

1½ gills of stock.

½ wineglass of port.

A tiny piece of carrot, turnip, and onion.

½ teaspoonful of anchovy sauce.

½ teaspoonful of Harvey's sauce.

Pepper and salt.

Method.—Melt the butter in a small stewpan, and fry the vegetables in it.
Then add the flour, and fry that.
Pour in the stock; stir and cook well.
Then add the wine and other ingredients,
Stir until it boils again, and then strain it.

Béchamel Sauce.

Ingredients—2 oz. of butter.

1½ oz. of flour.

1 pint of good white stock.

¼ pint of cream.

A few drops of lemon juice.

Pepper and salt.

Method.—Melt the butter in a stewpan.

Mix in the flour smoothly.

Add the stock.

Stir and cook well.

Then stir in the cream; let it boil in the sauce; and add lemon juice, pepper, and salt.

Strain through a tammy-cloth.

Milk may be substituted for the white stock, if more convenient. To flavour it, a small piece of carrot, turnip, and onion, and 6 button mushrooms should be boiled in it.

Sauce Hollandaise.

Ingredients—¼ pint of plain white sauce.

The yolks of 4 eggs.

A little cayenne pepper and salt.

A few drops of lemon juice, or taragon vinegar.

Method.—Put the white sauce and eggs into a jug, which must be placed in a saucepan of boiling water.

Stir until the mixture thickens, being careful it does not curdle.

When quite ready, add the lemon juice or vinegar.

Lobster Sauce.

Ingredients—1 small lobster.

Some spawn.

1½ oz. of butter.

1 oz. of flour.

½ pint of milk.

½ gill of cream.

A few drops of lemon juice.

Pepper and salt.

Method.—Remove the flesh from the body and claws of the lobster, and cut it in small pieces.

Then boil the shell, broken small, in the milk.

Rub the spawn with ¼ oz. butter through a hair sieve.

Melt the remaining butter in a small stewpan.

Mix in the flour smoothly, and then add the milk, strained.

Stir until it thickens.

Put in the spawn and butter, and continue stirring until the flour is well cooked.

Then add the cream—let it boil in the sauce—and lastly, the lemon juice, pepper and salt, and lobster.

Lobster Sauce (a plainer Receipt).

Ingredients—Part of a tin of lobster.

1 oz. of butter.

1 oz. of flour.

¾ pint of milk.

A few drops of lemon juice, or ½ a teaspoonful of vinegar.

Pepper and salt.

Method.—Cut up the lobster.

Melt the butter in a small stewpan.

Mix in the flour smoothly.

Add the milk; stir and cook well.

Then add the lemon juice, seasoning, and pieces of lobster.

Shrimp Sauce.

Remove the heads, tails, and skin from half a pint of shrimps; prepare some sauce as directed in the first or second recipe for lobster sauce, substituting the shrimps for the lobster.

Oyster Sauce.

Ingredients—1 oz. of butter.

1 oz. of flour.

½ pint of milk.

1 dozen of oysters.

½ gill of cream.

A few drops of lemon juice.

Salt, pepper, and a little cayenne.

Method.—Remove the beard and white part of the oysters, and cut each one in two.

Strain the liquor through muslin, and scald the oysters in it (*i.e.* put the liquor, with the oysters in it, in a saucepan, and just bring it to the boil).

Put the beards and hard white parts in the milk and simmer them to extract the flavour.

Then melt the butter in a small stewpan.

Mix in the flour smoothly.

Strain in the milk and oyster liquor, and stir and cook well.

Then add cream, and stir until the sauce again boils.

Lastly, add the oysters, pepper, salt, and lemon juice.

French Sauce.

Ingredients—1 oz. of butter.

½ oz. of flour.

1 gill of milk.

1 gill of cream.

The yolk of one egg.

Pepper and salt.

Method.—Melt the butter in a small stewpan.

Mix the flour smoothly.

Add the milk, stir and cook well.

Pour in the cream and let it boil in the sauce. Then take it off the fire, and mix in the yolk of the egg.

Add pepper and salt to taste.

Celery Sauce.

Ingredients—1 oz. of butter.

1 oz. of flour.

2 tablespoonfuls of cream.

¾ pint of white stock or milk.

1 head of celery.

Method.—Boil one head of celery in ¾ of a pint of white stock or milk.

When tender, strain it from the liquor and rub it through a hair sieve.

Melt the butter in a small stewpan.

Mix in the flour smoothly.

Add the stock or milk; stir and cook well.

Pour in the cream, and stir until the sauce boils again.

Add pepper and salt to taste.

Tomato Sauce.

Ingredients—6 ripe tomatoes.

¼ lb. of bacon.

1 oz. of flour.

A piece of carrot, turnip, and onion.

A sprig of parsley.

Thyme, marjoram, and a bay leaf.

A teaspoonful of vinegar.

Pepper and salt.

Method.—Cut the bacon in slices and fry it.

Then put in the vegetables and fry them, dredge in the flour, and then add the tomatoes and fry them lightly.

Empty the contents of the frying-pan on a hair sieve, and rub the tomatoes through. The hair sieve will keep back the other vegetable, the flavour of which only is wanted.

Add the vinegar and seasoning, and make the sauce hot.

Onion Sauce.

Ingredients—4 or 5 fair-sized onions.

½ pint of plain white sauce or melted butter (1st recipe).

Method.—First, blanch the onions by putting them in cold water and bringing it to the boil.

Throw the water away.

Put the onions in fresh water and boil for an hour, or an hour and a half, until tender.

Chop them finely and add them to the sauce or melted butter.

Soubise Sauce.

Ingredients—½ pint of plain white sauce.

2 tablespoonfuls of cream.

4 or 5 onions.

Method.—Blanch the onions (as in preceding recipe) and boil until tender.

Then rub through a hair sieve.

Make some plain white sauce (*see* recipe), and add to it the cream and pulped onion.

Bread Sauce.

Ingredients—2 oz. of bread crumbs.

½ pint of milk.

6 peppercorns.

2 tablespoonfuls of cream, or ½ oz. of butter.

A small piece of onion.

Method.—Steep the onion and peppercorns in the milk, and put the milk on to boil.

Then remove the onions and peppercorns, and sprinkle in the crumbs.

Set the sauce by the side of the fire for six minutes, and then heat to boiling point, adding either the cream or butter.

Salt must be added to taste; also a little cayenne.

Economical Family Sauce.

Ingredients—¼ lb. of flour.

1 pint of milk.

1 pint of water.

1½ oz. butter.

Method.—Mix the flour very smoothly with a little water.

Put the rest of the water, with the milk and butter, in a saucepan on the fire to boil.

When it boils, put in the flour, stirring until the sauce is cooked.

Add pepper and salt to taste. If liked, a few drops of lemon juice or vinegar may be added.

This sauce will form the basis of many other plain sauces: To use with fish, put in a tablespoonful of anchovy. Onion sauce is made by adding cooked and chopped onions when the sauce is ready. Caper sauce, by adding capers; or, as a substitute, chopped gherkin.

This sauce may be made still more economically by using water only instead of milk.

Wine Sauce.

Ingredients—1 oz. of lump sugar.

¼ pint of water.

A wineglass of sherry.

A few drops of cochineal.

A dessertspoonful of jam.

Method.—Boil the sugar and water together until reduced to one half.

Add the jam; let it melt.

Then add the sherry and cochineal, and strain.

Piquant Sauce.

Ingredients—½ pint of brown sauce.

1 tablespoonful of capers.

1 tablespoonful of chopped gherkin.

1 tablespoonful of very finely chopped shalot.

¼ pint of vinegar.

Pepper and salt.

Method.—Simmer the shalot, capers, and gherkin, in the vinegar until the shalot is quite soft.

Pour in the sauce, and let it boil up.

Season to taste.

Sauce Réforme.

Ingredients—1 pint of brown sauce.

1 wineglass of port wine.

1 teaspoonful of anchovy sauce.

1 teaspoonful of Harvey's sauce.

2 tablespoonfuls of red-currant jelly.

Method.—Boil all the ingredients together, and the sauce is ready.

Port-wine Sauce for Wild Duck.

Ingredients—2 wineglasses of port.

Juice of half a lemon.

1 finely chopped shalot.

Method.—Boil altogether and strain.

Sweet Sauce.

Ingredients—1 teaspoonful of arrowroot.

Juice of half a lemon and a little rind.

2 tablespoonfuls of castor sugar.

½ pint of water.

Method.—Put the water with the lemon-rind and sugar into a saucepan to boil.

Mix the arrowroot smoothly with a little cold water.

When the water in the saucepan boils, pour it in and stir it until it thickens; then strain it and add the lemon juice.

A glass of sherry may be added to this sauce if desired.

German Sauce.

Ingredients—The yolks of 2 eggs.

1 wineglass of sherry.

1 dessertspoonful of castor sugar.

Method.—Put all the ingredients into a saucepan, and mill over the fire with a whisk until the sauce froths.

For a *Christmas Pudding* make the sauce with three yolks, and a wineglass of brandy.

A Nice Sweet Sauce.

Ingredients—½ pint of plain white sauce or melted butter (omitting the seasoning).

1 wineglass of sherry or brandy.

2 dessertspoonfuls of castor sugar.

Method.—Add the wine and sugar to the sauce, and it is ready for use.

Jam Sauce.

Ingredients—3 tablespoonfuls of red jam.

½ pint of water.

1 oz. of lump sugar.

Juice of half a lemon.

Method.—Boil the jam, sugar, and water together for three minutes. Add the lemon juice, and strain.
The lemon may be omitted if the flavour is not liked.

Apple Sauce, No. 1.

Ingredients—6 good-sized apples.

1 oz. of butter.

1 tablespoonful of moist sugar, or more, according to taste.

½ gill of water.

Method.—Wash the apples and slice them, but do not peel or core them.
Put them in a stewpan with the water, butter, and sugar.
Stew gently for about thirty minutes, stirring occasionally.
Rub them quickly through a hair sieve, and put the sauce in a hot tureen.

The hair sieve keeps back the rind and pips.

Apple Sauce, No. 2.

Ingredients—6 large apples.

1 oz. of butter.

1 tablespoonful or more of moist sugar.

½ gill of water.

Method.—Peel, core, and slice the apples.

Stew them with the water, sugar, and butter until tender.

Then beat to a pulp with a fork.

Mint Sauce.

Ingredients—3 tablespoonfuls of finely-chopped fresh mint.

1 tablespoonful of sugar.

¼ pint of vinegar.

Method.—Mix all together, and let the sauce stand for an hour before serving.

Horse-radish Sauce.

Ingredients—1 stick of horse-radish.

½ gill of cream.

1 tablespoonful of vinegar.

½ gill of milk.

1 teaspoonful of ready-made mustard.

1 teaspoonful of castor sugar.

Pepper and salt.

Method.—Scrape the horse-radish finely, and mix with all the other ingredients.

If cream is not to be had, use milk thickened with a little cornflour. But it is not so good.

Gravy for Made Dishes.

Ingredients—1 lb. of gravy beef.

1 quart of water.

A piece of onion, carrot, and turnip.

1 sprig of parsley.

Thyme and marjoram.

Pepper and salt to taste.

Method.—Cut the beef into small pieces.

Put it with the vegetables into a stewpan with the water, and simmer very gently for four hours; then strain.

If a thick gravy is required, thicken with one and a half ounces of flour; add pepper and salt to taste.

To this gravy may be added a little sauce, catsup, port or sherry wine, &c., according to the purpose for which it is required.

Scraps of cooked meat and bones may be substituted for the fresh meat where economy must be studied.

Glaze.

Boil down one or two quarts of second stock (which will jelly when cold) until it is quite thick, and coats a spoon. One quart may be boiled down to a quarter of a pint.

Pour it into a jar.

When wanted for use, put the jar to stand in a saucepan of boiling water until it is dissolved.

Glaze is used for enriching gravies and soups, and for glazing meat.

Cheap Glaze for Meat.

Ingredients—3 teaspoonfuls of Liebig's Extract of Meat.

½ oz. of Nelson's or Swinborne's Gelatine, or isinglass.

Pepper and salt.

½ pint of cold water.

Method.—Soak the gelatine in the water for three-quarters of an hour.

Add the meat extract, and pepper and salt.

Stir and boil until reduced to about a quarter of a pint.

This glaze can only be used for glazing meat.

Béarnaise Sauce.

Ingredients—1 finely-chopped shalot.

½ gill of white sauce.

1 tablespoonful of taragon vinegar.

The yolks of 4 eggs.

1 dessertspoonful of finely-chopped parsley.

Pepper and salt.

Method.—Put the shalot and vinegar into a saucepan; boil until the vinegar has evaporated, but do not let the shalot burn.

Add the eggs and sauce, and mill with a whisk until the eggs are thick.

Add the parsley and pepper and salt.

BREAKFAST DISHES AND BEVERAGES.

Oatmeal Porridge.

Ingredients—½ lb. of coarse oatmeal.

1 quart of water.

Method.—Put the water on to boil.

When boiling, sprinkle in the oatmeal, stirring all the time.

When it thickens, put it by the side of the fire, and stir occasionally.

Cook it for quite three-quarters of an hour, longer if possible.

When the time can be allowed, three hours will not be too long a time, especially if the porridge is for anyone with a weak digestion.

A better plan is to put the saucepan containing it, after the contents have boiled for ten minutes, to stand in a saucepan of briskly boiling water; it will then cook without danger of burning, and may be left for any length of time; care only being taken that the water in the under saucepan does not boil away.

Whole-meal Porridge.

This may be made in the same way as oatmeal, but it requires even longer cooking.

Dry Toast.

Cut the bread into rather thin slices, and remove the crust.

Toast it slowly, holding it at a little distance from a bright clear fire.

When ready, put it at once into the rack; because, if the toast is placed flat on a table, it loses its crispness.

The crusts may be soaked for plain puddings, or dried and powdered for bread crumbs.

Buttered Toast.

Cut the bread about half an inch in thickness.

Toast quickly in front of a clear fire.

Put the butter on directly the toast is taken off the fork, and spread it quickly.

Put the toast on a *hot* plate, and take care that it is served hot.

Toasted Bacon.

Cut the bacon in thin slices, and toast it in a small Dutch oven or on a toasting fork until the fat is transparent.

Fried Bacon.

Cut the bacon in thin slices, and fry it in its own fat. It will be cooked when the fat is transparent. It must not be cooked too quickly, or the fat will burn up and be wasted.

Eggs and Bacon.

Toast or fry the bacon, and lay a nicely poached egg on each slice.

Boiled Eggs.

Put the eggs into boiling water, and boil an ordinary sized egg for three minutes; new-laid eggs will take one minute longer. Eggs boiled five minutes will be nearly hard. To make them quite firm, boil them steadily for ten minutes. To make them mealy, boil them for an hour.

Poached Eggs.

Eggs for poaching should be perfectly *fresh*, or they will not keep a nice shape.

Let the water be quite boiling; add to it a little salt.

Break the eggs into cups, and slip them gently into the boiling water.

As soon as the white is nicely set, remove them with a fish slice.

Trim the eggs neatly, and serve them on hot buttered toast.

An egg-poacher will be found very convenient for cooking eggs this way.

Fried Kidneys.

Ingredients—A few kidneys.

A little butter or dripping.

A little flour.

Some gravy.

Pepper and salt.

Method.—Split open the kidneys lengthwise.

Flour them and fry them slowly in the butter or dripping for about four minutes.

Dish them on pieces of toast.

Pour the gravy into the pan; stir and boil for a minute, and then strain round the kidneys.

Kidneys Toasted.

Ingredients—Some kidneys.

Toasted bread.

Method.—Split open the kidneys lengthwise.

Toast them before a clear fire; when the gravy ceases to drop red they will be sufficiently cooked.

A *hot* dish should be placed under them to catch the gravy.

Place the toast on the dish and put the kidneys on it, and sprinkle over them a little pepper and salt.

Stewed Kidneys.

Ingredients—2 or 3 kidneys.

½ pint of nice gravy.

1 dessertspoonful of flour.

Pepper and salt to taste.

Lemon juice.

Method.—Mix the flour smoothly with the gravy.

Put it into a stewpan, and boil well for three minutes.

Put in the kidneys cut in slices, and simmer gently for about fifteen minutes.

Add a squeeze of lemon juice; pepper and salt to taste.

Serve on a piece of toast, and pour the gravy over.

Stuffed Kidneys.

Ingredients—3 or 4 kidneys.

½ oz. of butter.

Half a shalot, chopped finely.

1 dessertspoonful of parsley.

1 tablespoonful of bread crumbs.

A few drops of lemon juice.

A little cayenne.

Pepper and salt.

Method.—Toast or broil the kidneys and split them open.

Fry the shalot in the butter.

Mix in the bread crumbs and parsley; add lemon juice, cayenne pepper, and salt.

Lay a little of the stuffing in each kidney and fold it over.

Serve very hot.

Kidneys à la Tartare.

Ingredients—A few kidneys.

½ pint of Tartare sauce.

Method.—Split the kidneys open, and toast or broil them nicely.

Serve on toasted bread with Tartare sauce in a tureen.

Fried Sausages.

Ingredients—Sausages.

A little butter or dripping.

Some toasted bread.

Method.—Prick the sausages with a fork, and fry them with butter or dripping, turning them that they get browned equally.

Serve them on toasted bread, with some nice gravy in a sauceboat.

Some people like the toast soaked in the fat in the pan, but this is a matter of taste.

Baked Sausages.

Prick the sausages, and place them on a greased baking-sheet.

Bake until they are nicely browned.

Serve on toast, with gravy in a sauceboat.

If liked, the toast can be soaked in the fat that runs from the sausages.

Oxford Sausages.

Remove the sausage-meat from the skins, and place it in little rough heaps on a greased baking-sheet.

Bake in a quick oven until browned.

Serve on toast.

Tomatoes stuffed with Sausage Meat.

Ingredients—Some nice ripe tomatoes.

Some sausage meat.

Method.—Cut the stalks from the tomatoes, but do not take out any of the inside.

Heap a little sausage meat on the top of each tomato.

Put them on a greased baking-sheet, and bake in a moderate oven for about fifteen minutes.

Croustards with Minced Meat.

Ingredients—Some stale bread.

Scraps of cold meat.

A little nice gravy.

A little mushroom catsup.

Pepper and salt to taste.

Method.—Cut the bread into slices three-quarters of an inch in thickness.

Stamp it into rounds with a circular cutter.

Mark the middle with a cutter two sizes smaller, and scoop out the inside, making little nests of them, and taking care not to break the bottom or sides.

Fry the cases in hot fat (*see* French Frying); drain them and put them inside the oven to keep hot.

Mince the meat nicely, removing skin and gristle.

Make a little gravy hot in a stewpan.

Put in the mince, and make it hot without letting it boil.

Flavour to taste with catsup, pepper and salt.

Fill the croustard cases and serve immediately: they should be placed on a folded napkin, and garnished with parsley.

Mince à la Reine.

Ingredients—1 dozen mushrooms.

Some slices of cold meat.

(Cold game or chicken are excellent for this purpose).

6 eggs.

Some rounds of bread, toasted or fried.

1 pint of good gravy.

Pepper and salt to taste.

Method.—Peel the mushrooms.

Wash and dry them well, and cut them in slices.

Put them in a stewpan with part of the gravy, to stew for about thirty minutes, until they are tender.

Mince the meat and make it hot in a saucepan, with enough gravy to moisten it, adding pepper and salt to taste.

Poach the eggs nicely, and fry or toast the bread (fried bread is best).

Put the slices of fried bread on a hot dish; cover each piece with the minced meat, and lay an egg on each.

Pour the gravy and mushrooms round, and serve very hot.

As a decoration, a tiny pinch of finely-chopped parsley might be put on the top of each egg.

Sheep's Head Moulded.

Ingredients—1 sheep's head.

2 hard-boiled eggs.

Pepper and salt.

Method.—Clean, and then boil the head until the flesh will leave the bones easily.

Take out all the bones; cut the meat into pieces an inch in size, and season them well with pepper and salt.

Cut the eggs into slices, and place them round the top of a cake-tin or basin.

Put in the head, and put a weight on it to press it down.

When cold turn it out; serve garnished with parsley.

Veal Cake.

Ingredients—Remains of cooked veal.

Slices of ham.

2 or 3 hard-boiled eggs.

Some nice second stock.

A little gelatine.

Some forcemeat balls.

Method.—Butter well a plain mould or basin.

Decorate it with slices of egg, and balls made of veal forcemeat.

Cut the ham and the veal into neat pieces.

Season them well with pepper and salt, and, if liked, a little chopped parsley.

Place them in the mould, and fill it up with stiff second stock.

If the stock is not stiff enough, mix with it a little melted gelatine.

Cover the mould, and bake for one hour in a moderate oven.

Let it get cold, and then turn it on to a dish.

Brawn.

Ingredients—1 pig's head.

2 or 3 hard-boiled eggs.

2 onions.

6 cloves.

1 blade of mace.

2 dozen peppercorns.

1 sprig of parsley, thyme, and marjoram.

Method.—Clean the head well, and pickle it for three days (*see* Pickle for Meat).

Then put it in enough cold water to cover it, and boil it gently for three hours or more, until the flesh will leave the bones easily.

Take out the tongue, skin it, and cut it in slices.

Stamp them into fancy shapes with a paste cutter; wet a plain round mould and decorate it with them and the eggs cut in slices.

Remove the meat from the bone, and cut it into large dice.

Take one quart of the liquor in which the head was boiled; put the bones into it, with the peppercorns, cloves, onions, and herbs; boil down for half an hour with the lid off the saucepan.

Then strain one pint of the broth into another saucepan.

Season the pieces of meat with pepper, and a little salt if necessary; put them into the broth.

Let it come to the boil, and then pour it into the decorated mould.

When set, turn it on to a dish.

Scalloped Eggs.

Ingredients—Some eggs.

Bread-crumbs.

A little onion, chopped as finely as possible (this may be omitted, if liked).

A little finely-chopped parsley.

Pepper and salt to taste.

Method.—Grease some deep scallop shells.

Dust them over with bread crumbs, mixed with the parsley and onion.

Put an egg into each shell, and sprinkle with more crumbs, parsley, onion, pepper and salt.

Put them into a brisk oven until set.

Eggs sur le Plat.

Ingredients—4 eggs.

½ oz. of butter.

Pepper and salt.

Method.—Take a dish that will stand the heat of the oven; melt the butter in it.

Break the eggs on to it very carefully.

Pepper and salt them, and put them into the oven until they are set.

They must be served on the same dish.

Buttered Eggs.

Ingredients—1 piece of fried or toasted bread.

1 tablespoonful of gravy.

1 oz. of butter.

Pepper and salt.

4 eggs.

Method.—Break the eggs into a basin, and add to them the gravy, pepper, and salt.

Melt the butter in a small frying or omelet pan; pour in the eggs, and stir quickly up from the bottom of the pan, until the whole is a soft yellow mass.

Spread on the toast, and serve very quickly.

Egg Croustards.

Ingredients—Some slices of stale bread, about ¾ inch in thickness.

Some eggs.

Some nicely-flavoured gravy.

Method.—Stamp out some rounds of bread with a circular paste-cutter.

Mark the middle with one a size smaller.

Then with a knife scoop out the inside, making little nests of bread, taking care not to break the bottom or sides.

Fry these cases in hot fat (*see* French Frying).

When fried, drain them on kitchen paper, and keep them hot.

Make some water boiling hot in a stewpan; add to it a little lemon juice.

Put into it the eggs broken gently into cups.

Poach until the whites are set, then remove them carefully with a fish slice, and put an egg into each croustard.

Place them on a hot dish, and pour gravy boiling hot over them.

Eggs and Anchovy.

Ingredients—2 eggs.

1 slice of fried or toasted bread.

A little anchovy paste.

1 oz. of butter.

Pepper and salt to taste.

Method.—Let the fried or toasted bread be quite hot (fried bread is the best), and spread it thinly with anchovy paste.

Make the butter quite hot in a frying or omelet pan.

Break the eggs into it, add pepper and salt, and stir very quickly, until they are a soft yellow mass.

Spread it quickly over the toast, and serve immediately.

Eggs in Cases.

Ingredients—4 tablespoonfuls of bread crumbs.

1 dessertspoonful of finely-chopped parsley.

Pepper and salt.

If liked, a boiled onion very finely chopped.

6 eggs.

6 paper cases.

Method.—Butter well some paper cases; mix the crumbs, parsley, onion, pepper, and salt together; put a little at the bottom of each case.

Break the eggs gently, and put one egg into each case.

Cover each with some of the crumbs and seasoning, and put the cases in a quick oven to bake until the eggs are set.

Broiled Mushrooms.

Choose nice large mushrooms; peel and wash them, and wipe them dry.

Cut out the stems, and put them, with the top of the mushrooms downwards, on a gridiron.

Put a small piece of butter on each, and broil for ten minutes slowly.

Remove them carefully, as the mushrooms will be by that time full of delicious gravy.

Broiled Dried Haddock.

Soak it in cold water for an hour before using.

Broil it slowly over a clear fire until it is quite hot, turning occasionally.

Rub some butter over it, and serve it at once.

Bloaters.

Cut the bloaters open down the back, and bone them.

Lay them one on the other with the insides together.

Broil them slowly over a clear fire, turning occasionally.

Serve very hot, with a little butter rubbed over them.

If preferred, they may be broiled unboned.

Red Herrings.

Remove their heads and tails.

Slit them open down the back and remove the bone.

Egg and bread-crumb them, and broil them over a clear fire.

If preferred, they may be broiled unboned.

Tea.

Measure a teaspoonful of tea for each person, and one teaspoonful over.

Make the teapot quite hot by filling it with boiling water; let it stand in it for three minutes; then empty the teapot.

Put in the tea, and pour boiling water over it.

Cover it with a tea-cosy, and let it infuse for five minutes before using. The longer it stands, the darker it will get; but for people of weak digestions, it should be used after five minutes' infusion only.

The water should be fresh spring water, and should be used as soon as it boils. Water that has been boiled for any length of time is flat from the loss of its gases.

Coffee.

To have coffee to perfection it should be freshly roasted and ground, as coffee quickly loses its flavour. If this is not possible, use the best French coffee sold in tins. The water should be freshly boiled; the coffee itself should *not* be *boiled,* but only infused in the boiling water. Boiling disperses the aroma. It can, however, be made more economically if boiled, and therefore recipes are given for its preparation in this manner. Chicory is generally used with coffee in the proportion of two ounces of chicory to one pound of coffee.

Coffee (Soyer's method.)

Ingredients—3 oz. of coffee.
1 pint of boiling water.
Method.—Put the coffee into a clean stewpan.
Stir over the fire until it smokes, but do not let it burn.
Then pour in the boiling water.
Cover close, and set by the side of the fire for ten minutes.
Strain through thick muslin.

Coffee (another method).

Ingredients—3 oz. of coffee.
1½ pint of boiling water.

Method.—Make a jug hot.

Put the coffee in it, and pour over the boiling water.

Let it stand in a hot place for half an hour.

Then strain through thick muslin.

Café au Lait.

Half fill a cup with nicely-made coffee, and pour in the same quantity of boiled milk.

Coffee (economical method).

Ingredients—¾ lb. of coffee.

2 quarts of cold water.

Method.—Make a bag of rather thick muslin, and put the coffee into it. The bag should be rather large, so that the coffee will have plenty of room.

Tie the ends of the bag securely.

Put it into a saucepan with the water; bring to the boil, and boil steadily for one hour.

Strain through thick muslin.

This will make strong coffee, which can be diluted with boiling water as required.

Coffee made in a Percolator.

Ingredients—3 oz. of coffee.

1½ pint of boiling water.

Method.—Make the percolator hot.

Put the coffee in it, and pour on the boiling water.

Let it stand in a hot place for about ten minutes.

Cocoa.

This is best, especially for invalids, if prepared from the nibs; these should be perfectly fresh.

Put a quarter of a pound of nibs into two quarts of cold water; simmer for five hours and then strain.

When cold remove the fat; heat it as required.

Cocoa may also be made from any of the different preparations.

Make it according to directions given on the canisters, and be very careful to mix it thoroughly. Nothing is so unpleasant as to have the sides and bottom of the cup coated with cocoa.

It is better to prepare it in a small saucepan; it should be boiled for two or three minutes.

It is more nourishing if mixed with milk instead of water.

Chocolate.

This is only a thicker preparation of cocoa, and may be made in the same way.

COLD MEAT COOKERY.

Hash.

Ingredients—The remains of cold meat.

Some nice stock or gravy.

Flour, in the proportion of ½ oz. to every ½ pint of gravy.

Pepper and salt, and, if liked, a little catsup, or Harvey's sauce.

Toasted or fried bread.

Method.—Cut the meat into neat pieces.

Mix the flour smoothly with the gravy, and boil for three minutes, stirring all the time.

Add seasoning and catsup or a little sauce.

Then put the pieces of meat into the gravy and let them warm through; but do not let the gravy *boil* when the meat is in it, as that would toughen it.

Tinned oysters make a nice addition to a hash.

For serving, put the hash on a hot dish and garnish with sippets of fried or toasted bread.

If no gravy or stock is available, make some by breaking up any bones from the meat; boil them in a sufficient quantity of water, with a piece of carrot, turnip, onion, celery, and a small bunch of herbs.

Boil for quite an hour, and then strain the liquor.

Minced Meat.

Ingredients—Some scraps of cold meat.

A little gravy.

Some boiled rice or potatoes.

Pepper and salt to taste.

Method.—Mince the meat finely with a knife, or mincing machine (the flavour is nicer if a knife is used).

Mix with sufficient gravy to moisten the meat, and stir over the fire until hot; but do not let the gravy boil.

Serve with a border of boiled rice, or mashed potatoes round it.

If veal or chicken is minced, squeeze in a few drops of lemon juice, and serve with sliced lemon.

A little cooked ham should be added to these minces, to give them flavour; minced beef is improved by the addition of a few oysters.

Mince (with Eggs).

Prepare some mince, as in preceding recipe, and serve with very nicely poached eggs on the top of it; garnish with sippets of fried or toasted bread.

Curry of Cold Meat.

Ingredients—Some scraps of cold meat.

Some stock or gravy.

Curry powder and flour in the proportion of a dessertspoonful of each to every half pint of gravy.

1 small onion.

1 small apple.

½ oz. of dripping.

A few drops of lemon juice.

Salt.

Some boiled rice.

Method.—Slice the onion and apple, and fry them in the dripping.

When fried, rub them lightly through a hair sieve.

Mix the curry powder and flour smoothly with the stock.

Stir and cook well over the fire.

Add the onion, apple, lemon juice, and salt.

Then lay in the meat, and let it warm through, being careful that the sauce does not boil.

Serve with nicely boiled rice.

Shepherd's Pie.

Ingredients—Slices of cold meat.

Boiled potatoes.

Butter or dripping.

A little gravy.

Pepper and salt.

Method.—Season the pieces of meat with pepper and salt, and lay them in a pie-dish with a little gravy.

Mash the potatoes smoothly with butter or dripping; and pepper and salt to taste.

Spread the potatoes over the meat in the form of a pie-crust, and smooth them with a knife dipped in hot water.

Bake for half an hour.

Patties.

Ingredients—Some scraps of cold meat.

A little gravy.

Pepper and salt.

Pastry.

1 egg.

Method.—Mince the meat and moisten with the gravy, adding pepper and salt to taste.

If veal or chicken are used, mince a little ham with them, and add a few drops of lemon juice.

Roll out the pastry, and stamp it into rounds with a fluted cutter.

Lay half the rounds on greased pattypans.

Brush round the edges of the paste with a little beaten egg, and put a little mince on each round.

Cover them with the remaining rounds of paste, pressing the edges lightly together.

Glaze with the beaten egg, and bake in a quick oven for about 15 minutes.

Fritters.

Ingredients—Some cold meat.

Some nice gravy.

Some Kromesky batter.

Method.—Cut the meat into neat pieces; dip them in the batter and fry in hot fat until lightly browned (*see* French Frying).

Pile on a hot dish, and serve, if possible, with a nice gravy poured round them.

Rissoles.

Ingredients—Some boiled potatoes.

Cold meat.

A little butter.

2 eggs.

Bread-crumbs.

Pepper and salt.

Method.—Take equal quantities of boiled potatoes and cold meat.

Mash the potatoes with butter, and add the meat finely minced.

Mix this thoroughly with a beaten egg, adding pepper and salt to taste.

Form into balls or egg shapes.

Egg and bread-crumb them, and fry them in hot fat (*see* French Frying).

Dish on a folded napkin, and garnish with fried parsley.

Cold Meat with Purée of Tomatoes.

Ingredients—Slices of cold meat.

4 or 5 tomatoes.

1 small slice of bacon.

1 bay leaf.

1 piece of carrot, turnip, and onion.

1 sprig of parsley.

Thyme and marjoram.

1 teaspoonful of vinegar.

Pepper and salt.

Method.—Cut the bacon into dice, and fry it.

As soon as the fat melts, put in the tomatoes and other vegetables, cut in slices; stir them, and fry lightly, and then rub through a hair sieve.

Add the vinegar and pepper and salt.

Make the *purée* hot in a saucepan, and lay the pieces of meat in it to warm through.

Serve in a hot dish, with a border of boiled rice or macaroni.

Cold-meat Pie.

Ingredients—Slices of cold meat.

(If liked, slices of cold boiled potatoes).

Some stock or gravy.

Pepper and salt.

Some plain pastry.

Method.—Roll out the paste, and cut a piece large enough for the cover.

Roll out the scraps, and from them cut a band an inch wide.

Wet the edge of the dish and place this round it.

Season the meat with pepper and salt, and lay the slices in the dish alternately with the potatoes.

Raise them in the middle of the dish in a dome-like shape, and pour in some gravy.

Wet the edges of the band of paste, and lay the cover over.

Trim round neatly, and make a hole in the middle of the crust.

Brush over with beaten egg, and decorate with paste leaves.

Bake in a quick oven for half an hour.

Cold Meat and Macaroni.

Ingredients—Slices of cold meat.

Macaroni.

Stock.

Bread-crumbs.

And, if possible, 2 or 3 tomatoes.

Method.—Put the macaroni in boiling water, and boil it 20 minutes.

Then pour away the water, and stew it in the stock until tender.

Put a layer of macaroni in the bottom of a greased pie-dish.

Lay on it the meat, and cover it with another layer of macaroni, seasoning with pepper and salt.

Proceed in this way, until the dish is full (the top layer must be macaroni).

If tomatoes are used, slice them, and lay over the top; sprinkle with brown crumbs, and bake for about 20 or 30 minutes.

Mayonnaise of Cold Meat.

Ingredients—Slices of cold meat.

Green salad.

Beetroot.

Hard-boiled egg.

Some Mayonnaise sauce.

Method.—Slice the salad, and mix the meat with it.

Heap it high on a glass or silver dish.

Garnish with beetroot and hard-boiled egg, and pour Mayonnaise sauce over (*see* Sauces).

Beef and Mushrooms.

Ingredients—1½ lb. cold roast beef.

1 dozen mushrooms.

1 shalot or small onion, very finely chopped.

2 oz. of butter.

½ pint of beef gravy.

1 dessertspoonful of vinegar.

Pepper and salt to taste.

Method.—Cut the beef into neat slices, and wash and peel the mushrooms.

Season the meat with pepper and salt, and lay half of it in the bottom of a pie-dish.

Place some of the mushrooms on the top of it.

Put 1 oz. of butter, in pieces, about them.

Then put in the remaining pieces of beef, and the mushrooms and butter in the same way.

Pour in the gravy and vinegar, and cover closely.

Put it into a moderate oven to bake for three-quarters of an hour.

Beef Scalloped.

Ingredients—Some cold roast beef minced.

1 boiled onion, very finely chopped.

Some mashed potatoes.

Butter.

Pepper and salt.

1 egg.

A little gravy and mushroom catsup.

Method.—Mince the beef finely, and moisten it with a little nice gravy.

Add the onion to it, and season nicely with catsup.

Mix the mashed potatoes with plenty of butter, and the egg well beaten, pepper and salt.

Place the mince in greased scallop shells, and cover with the potatoes.

Bake in a quick oven until lightly browned.

When economy has to be studied, leave out the eggs and substitute clarified dripping for the butter. The mixture can be baked in a pie-dish, if more convenient.

Cold Beef Olives.

Ingredients—Some cold roast beef.

Some veal forcemeat, omitting the suet.

Some gravy.

Flour.

Pepper and salt.

Some mashed potatoes.

Method.—Take slices of cold beef, and cut them into strips 1½ inches in width.

Lay on each a little veal stuffing; roll them round it, and tie them with string.

Put them into a stewpan close together; pour the gravy over them, and simmer them gently for ten minutes.

Dish them on a border of mashed potatoes.

Thicken the gravy with a little flour, and pour it over them.

ENTRÉES.

Quenelles of Veal.

Ingredients—1 lb. of fillet of veal.

1 oz. of butter.

2 oz. of flour.

1 gill of water.

A few drops of lemon juice.

2 eggs.

Seasoning.

Method.—Scrape the veal finely.

Melt the butter in a saucepan; mix in the flour.

Then add the water and cook well.

Put this panada into a mortar with the veal, eggs, lemon juice, and seasoning, and pound thoroughly.

Then rub through a wire sieve.

Shape the mixture somewhat like eggs with dessertspoons and a knife dipped in hot water.

Poach them gently in a greased frying-pan, or *sauté* pan, for ten minutes.

Dish them on a border of mashed potatoes, and pour white sauce over them.

Garnish with chopped truffle and ham.

Cooked green peas, mushrooms, or other vegetables, may be placed in the centre.

Mutton Cutlets à la Macédoine.

Ingredients—Part of best end of neck of mutton.

1 egg.

Bread-crumbs.

3 oz. of clarified butter.

Seasoning.

Method.—Saw off the chine bone, and the ends of the rib bones, leaving the cutlet bone three inches in length.

Cut the cutlets with a bone to each, and beat them with a cutlet bat to about half an inch in thickness.

Trim them, and leave half an inch of the rib bone bare.

Season, egg and bread-crumb, and fry in clarified butter in a *sauté* pan for five or seven minutes.

Dish on a border of mashed potatoes, put a *macédoine* of vegetables in the centre, and pour brown sauce round them.

Mutton Cutlets à la Rachel.

Ingredients—Some mutton cutlets.

Foie gras.

Brown sauce.

Macédoine of vegetables.

Mashed potatoes.

Truffle.

Pigs' caul.

Method.—Plainly fry some mutton cutlets, coat one side of each cutlet with the *foie gras*, smoothing it with a knife dipped in hot water.

Lay a small piece of truffle on each cutlet and cover them with pigs' caul.

Put them on a baking-sheet in a moderate oven for about a quarter of an hour.

Dish them on a border of mashed potatoes.

Pour brown sauce round them, and put a *macédoine* of vegetables in the middle.

Epigrammes.

Ingredients—The rib part, which was sawn off the mutton cutlets.

Egg and bread-crumbs.

Method.—Boil the mutton until the bones can be easily removed.

Press it, and, when cold, cut it into cutlets or other shapes.

Egg and bread-crumb twice, and fry in hot fat (345°) in a frying-basket.

Dish on a border of mashed potatoes, and pour brown sauce round them.

Any cooked vegetables can be put in the centre for a garnish.

Chicken Croquettes.

Ingredients—2 oz. of cooked chicken.
1 oz. of cooked ham.
1 oz. of butter.
¾ oz. of flour.
1 gill of stock.
½ gill of cream.
6 button mushrooms.
A few drops of lemon juice.
Seasoning.
Pastry.

Method.—Mince the chicken, ham, and mushrooms.
Melt the butter in a small stewpan.
Mix in the flour.
Pour in the stock, and cook well.

Then add cream, lemon juice, and seasoning; lastly, the chicken, ham, and mushrooms.

Spread on a plate to cool.
Roll out some paste as thin as possible.
Cut into rounds.
Put a little of the mixture on each, and egg round the edges.

Fold them over, egg and bread-crumb the *croquettes,* and fry in a frying-basket in hot fat (*see* French Frying).

Garnish with fried parsley.

Veal Cutlets à la Talleyrand.

Ingredients—7 or 8 veal cutlets.

1½ oz. butter.

3 button mushrooms, chopped.

1 small shalot, chopped.

A teaspoonful of chopped parsley.

The yolks of 2 eggs.

2 tablespoonfuls of cream.

A few drops of lemon juice.

1 gill of white sauce (*see* Sauces).

Some mashed potatoes.

A few green peas.

Pepper and salt.

Method.—Fry the cutlets in the butter, sprinkling the mushroom, shalot, and parsley under and over them.

When the cutlets are cooked, remove them from the pan and pour in the white sauce and cream.

Stir briskly over the fire.

Then add the yolks of the eggs; let them thicken in the sauce, but be careful not to curdle them.

Take the pan off the fire, and add the lemon juice and seasoning as required.

Dish the cutlets on a border of mashed potatoes.

Pour the sauce over them, and put a few nicely cooked peas, or other appropriate vegetables, in the middle.

Fillets of Beef à la Béarnaise.

Ingredients—7 or 8 nice little fillets.

1½ oz. of butter.

Mashed potatoes.

½ pint of brown sauce (*see* Sauces), or good gravy.

Some good *Béarnaise* sauce (*see* Sauces).

Method.—Fry the fillets in the butter.

Dish them on a border of mashed potatoes.

Pour brown sauce or gravy round them, and put the *Béarnaise* sauce in the middle of the fillets.

Rabbits à la Tartare.

Ingredients—1 rabbit.

Some browned bread-crumbs.

1 egg.

½ pint of Tartare sauce (*see* Sauces).

Method.—Cut the rabbit into joints.

Dry them well.

Egg and bread-crumb them.

Put them on a greased baking-sheet, with pieces of butter on them.

Bake for half an hour, being careful not to dry them up too much.

Pour the sauce on a dish and pile up the rabbit in the middle of it.

Chicken à la Tartare.

Proceed as in the foregoing recipe, substituting a chicken for a rabbit.

Pigeons Stewed à l'Italienne.

Ingredients—3 pigeons.

1 piece of carrot, turnip, and onion.

1 pint of stock.

1 sprig of parsley, thyme, and marjoram.

1 bay leaf.

If possible, 1 or 2 tomatoes.

1 wineglass of sherry.

2 oz. of butter.

1 oz. of flour.

Some mashed potatoes.

A *macédoine* of vegetables.

Method.—Have the pigeons trussed as for stewing.

Cut them in two, and fry them in the butter.

Then remove the pigeons, and fry the vegetables.

Stir the flour, and when that is a little brown, pour in the stock or sherry. Put in the pigeons and stew gently until they are tender.

Dish them in a circle on a border of mashed potatoes.

Strain the gravy over, and put a *macédoine* of vegetables in the centre.

Croustards à la Reine.

Ingredients—Some puff pastry.

A little *quenelle* meat (*see* Quenelles of Veal).

1 gill of white sauce.

3 oz. of cold chicken minced.

1 oz. of cooked ham minced.

2 or 3 button mushrooms finely chopped.

2 tablespoonfuls of cream.

A little thick white sauce.

Ham or truffle for decoration.

Method.—Line some little tartlet tins with some puff paste, put a piece of dough in each, and bake them.

Mix the chicken, ham, and mushrooms with the white sauce and cream. Add pepper and salt to taste.

Remove the paste cases from the tins, take the dough from the middle, and fill them with the chicken mixture.

Cover the top of each with the *quenelle* meat spread like butter, put them into the oven for a few minutes to cook the *quenelle* meat.

When dishing them up, spread a little thick white sauce on the top of each, and ornament them with ham and truffle.

Sweetbreads à la Béchamel.

Ingredients—1 dozen lambs' heart sweetbreads.

1¼ pint of veal stock.

1 oz. of butter.

1 oz. of flour.

A small piece of carrot, turnip, and onion.

1 sprig of parsley.

2 tablespoonfuls of cream.

A slice of lean ham.

A few drops of lemon juice.

Some mashed potatoes.

A few green peas nicely boiled.

A little finely-chopped cooked ham.

Some parsley or truffle.

Pepper and salt.

Method.—Trim the sweetbreads, and soak them in cold water for two hours.

Then throw them into boiling water, and simmer them gently for five minutes.

Soak them again in cold water for twenty minutes.

Then put them in a stewpan with the stock, carrot, turnip, onion, parsley, and ham.

Simmer gently until the sweetbreads are quite tender.

Then remove them, and add to the stock the flour mixed thoroughly with butter.

Stir and boil well, to cook the flour.

Add the cream, lemon juice, and seasoning.

Strain the sauce through a fine strainer or tammy-cloth.

Dish the sweetbreads in a circle on a border of mashed potatoes.

Pour the sauce over them.

Put on each sweetbread a tiny pinch of finely-chopped parsley, ham, or truffle; or use all three, placing them alternately.

The green peas should be put in the centre of the dish.

Braised Sweetbreads.

Ingredients—2 calves' sweetbreads.

1 pint of strong second stock.

A piece of carrot, turnip, and onion.

1 sprig of parsley, thyme, and marjoram.

1 bay leaf.

Some larding bacon.

Some carrots and turnips cut in fancy shapes.

Method.—Soak the sweetbreads in cold water for quite two hours.

Then put them in boiling water, and simmer them for ten minutes to make them firm.

Soak them again in cold water for twenty minutes, and then lard them nicely.

Put the vegetables, cut in pieces, in the bottom of a stewpan.

Lay the sweetbreads on them, and pour in the stock; it should come half way up the sweetbreads.

Cover them with buttered paper, and put the lid on the stewpan.

Simmer gently until the sweetbreads are tender.

Then put them on a baking-tin, and put them in the oven to brown.

Strain the stock they were cooked in into a large saucepan, and boil it rapidly down to a glaze.

Put the sweetbreads on a hot dish, and pour the glaze over.

Carrots and turnips may be cut in fancy shapes, and nicely boiled to garnish the dish.

If preferred, the sweetbreads can be cooked without being larded; a slice of very thin bacon being laid on the top of each.

If a proper braising-pan is used, the sweetbreads need not be browned in the oven.

Lambs' sweetbreads can be cooked the same way. One dozen will be wanted for a small dish.

Sweetbreads à la Parisienne.

Ingredients—1 dozen lambs' heart sweetbreads.

1 pint of good second stock.

2 oz. of butter.

1 oz. of flour.

A piece of carrot, turnip, and onion.

1 sprig of parsley.

1 dessertspoonful of mushroom catsup.

1 wineglass of sherry.

A few drops of lemon juice.

Pepper and salt.

Some mashed potatoes.

Green peas nicely cooked.

Method.—Trim the sweetbreads and soak them for two hours; throw them in boiling water, and simmer them gently for five minutes; then soak them in cold water for twenty minutes.

Simmer them in the stock until they are quite tender.

Then make the butter quite hot in a stewpan.

Fry the sweetbreads in it until nicely browned.

Remove them and fry the flour; then pour in the stock, and stir, and cook well; add the catsup, wine, and lemon juice.

Dish the sweetbreads on a border of mashed potatoes, and pour the same over them.

Put a garnish of nicely cooked green peas in the middle.

Minced Sweetbread.

Ingredients—The remains of dressed sweetbreads.

2 or 3 mushrooms.

Enough stock to moisten nicely.

1 teaspoonful of flour.

A slice of cooked ham.

A few drops of lemon juice.

1 oz. of butter.

Pepper and salt.

Method.—Mince the sweetbreads, mushrooms, and ham.

Melt the butter in a stewpan, and fry the mushrooms in it.

Put in the flour, and mix it smoothly with the butter.

Then put in the sweetbread and ham, and enough stock to mix nicely.

Add lemon juice, pepper, and salt, to taste.

Make it hot, and then put the mixture into oiled-paper cases.

Sprinkle over the top of each a few browned crumbs and put in the oven for a few minutes.

Fried Sweetbread.

Ingredients—1 dozen lambs' heart sweetbreads.

1 pint of good stock.

1 oz. of butter.

1 oz. of flour.

A few drops of lemon juice.

If liked, ½ wineglass of sherry.

Eggs and bread-crumbs.

Some mashed potatoes and green peas.

Method.—Trim the sweetbreads, and soak them in cold water for two hours.

Then throw them into the boiling stock, and simmer them for half an hour or more until quite tender.

If possible, let them get cold in the stock.

Then egg and bread-crumb them, and fry them in a frying basket in hot fat (*see* French Frying).

To make a sauce, melt the butter in a saucepan.

Mix in the flour smoothly, pour in the stock, and stir and cook well; add lemon juice, pepper, and salt to taste, and, if liked, a little sherry.

Dish the sweetbreads on the potatoes; pour the sauce round them, and put the peas in the centre.

The sauce should be made before the sweetbreads are fried, that there may be no delay in serving.

If calves' sweetbreads are used, proceed in the same way, cutting them in neat slices before frying.

Cutlets of Veal with Tomato Sauce.

Ingredients—2 lb. of fillet of veal.

2 or 3 oz. of butter, or some of the fat skimmed from the stock-pot.

1 pint of tomato sauce.

¼ lb. macaroni, nicely stewed in milk and seasoned with Parmesan cheese.

Some mashed potatoes.

1 uncooked tomato.

Method.—Cut the veal into neat little cutlets, and fry them nicely in the butter or skimming.

Dish them in a circle on a border of potatoes.

Pile the macaroni high in the middle.

Pour tomato sauce round, and garnish the macaroni with small strips of uncooked tomato.

Beef Olives.

Ingredients—1½ lb. of thick beefsteak.

Some veal stuffing.

1½ pint of stock.

1 oz. of butter.

1 oz. of flour.

A few drops of lemon juice.

Pepper and salt.

Some mashed potatoes.

A few carrots and turnips, cut in fancy shapes, and nicely cooked.

Method.—Cut the beef into thin strips, lay a little forcemeat on each, and roll them up.

Tie each roll with a little fine string.

Put them in a stewpan close together, and cover them with the stock.

Stew them gently for two or three hours until quite tender.

Then place them in a circle on a border of mashed potatoes.

Remove any fat from the stock, and stir in the butter and flour thoroughly mixed together.

Cook the flour well, and then add the lemon juice and seasoning.

Strain the sauce over the olives, and put the vegetables in the centre.

Veal à la Béchamel.

Ingredients—1 lb. of cold cooked veal.

¼ lb. of button mushrooms.

½ pint of *Béchamel* sauce.

The yolks of 2 eggs.

Some fried sippets of bread.

Method.—Cut the veal into large dice.

Clean the mushrooms and stew them in the sauce until tender.

Then add the yolks of two eggs well beaten.

Stir over the fire until they thicken, but on no account let the sauce *boil*, as that might curdle the eggs.

Last of all, put in the pieces of veal, and let the saucepan remain by the fire until they are thoroughly heated.

Serve garnished with fried sippets of bread.

Grenadines of Veal.

Ingredients—2 lb. of veal.

Some larding bacon.

Some good second stock.

1 piece of carrot, turnip, onion.

1 sprig of parsley, thyme, and marjoram.

Some nicely boiled green peas.

Method.—Cut the fillet into nice oval-shaped cutlets, about half an inch in thickness, and lard them.

Put the vegetables, cut in small pieces, at the bottom of the stewpan.

Lay the cutlets on them, and pour in sufficient stock to come half way up the cutlets.

Cover them with buttered paper, and put them on a slow fire to simmer gently until tender.

Then put them on a baking-tin in the oven to brown.

Strain the stock and boil it with a half-pint more to a strong glaze.

Dish the *grenadines* on a border of mashed potatoes.

Pour a little glaze over each, and put the green peas in the middle.

Mayonnaise of Fowl.

Cold Entrée for Suppers.

Ingredients—2 fowls.

½ pint of *mayonnaise* sauce.

A cucumber.

4 hard-boiled eggs.

1 pint of aspic jelly.

A beetroot.

Method.—Boil the fowls and cut them into neat joints.

Put them in a dish in a circle, the one leaning on the other.

Place in the middle a bunch of endive, and coat the pieces of chicken with *mayonnaise* sauce.

Cut the hard-boiled eggs in quarters, and lay them round the chicken with slices of cucumber and beetroot, and garnish with a border of chopped aspic.

Veal Cutlets.

Ingredients—2 lb. of veal cutlet.

Egg and bread-crumbs.

3 oz. of clarified butter.

½ oz. of flour.

½ pint of nice stock.

Some mashed potatoes.

Method.—Beat the cutlet well to break the fibre of the meat, and then cut it into neat oval or round shapes.

Brush them with the egg and cover them with fine bread-crumbs.

Fry them in a cutlet-pan in the butter.

When they are cooked pour some of the butter from the pan.

Stir in the flour smoothly.

Pour in the stock, and cook well.

Add pepper and salt and a few drops of lemon juice.

Dish the cutlets in a circle on a border of mashed potatoes.

Strain the gravy round them, and put some nice little rolls of bacon in the middle.

To cook the bacon, cut it in thin slices; roll them, and put them on a skewer, they may be either toasted or baked.

Veal Cutlets à l'Italienne.

Ingredients—1½ lb. of fillet of veal.

Cut into neat cutlets.

2 oz. of butter.

Egg and bread-crumbs.

Some carrot and turnip, cut in fancy shapes and boiled.

½ pint of Italian sauce.

Method.—Egg and bread-crumb the cutlets and fry them in the butter.

Dish them on a border of mashed potatoes.

Pour Italian sauce over, and put the vegetables in the middle.

Make the Italian sauce with the butter the cutlets are fried in.

Fillets of Chicken.

Ingredients—Some little fillets of chicken cut from the breast.

Some streaky bacon.

½ pint of *Béchamel* sauce, made with white stock.

Some mashed potatoes.

Method.—Lay the fillet on a greased baking-tin.

Cover with buttered paper and put them into a moderate oven for ten or fifteen minutes.

Dish them on a border of mashed potatoes.

Pour the sauce over and put little rolls of nicely cooked bacon in the middle.

To cook the bacon, cut it into very thin strips and roll them, run a skewer through, and toast them before the fire.

Chicken à la Marengo.

Ingredients—1 chicken.

1½ pint of second stock.

3 tomatoes.

1 piece of carrot, turnip, and onion.

1 sprig of parsley, thyme, marjoram.

2 oz. of butter.

1 oz. of flour.

A few drops of lemon juice.

Method.—Cut the chicken into neat joints and fry them in the butter.

Then remove them and fry the vegetables.

Add the flour and fry that.

Then pour in the stock; stir and boil for three minutes.

Then put in the chicken and the tomato, sliced.

Simmer for about thirty minutes, until the chicken is quite tender.

Then put the chicken on to an *entrée* dish.

Add some lemon juice to the gravy, and strain over it.

Chicken à la Cardinal.

Ingredients—1 chicken.

1½ pint of *Béchamel* sauce.

4 ripe tomatoes.

Method.—Cut the chicken into joints and put them in a stewpan with the sauce and tomatoes, sliced.

Simmer gently until the chicken is quite tender.

Then place them on a hot *entrée* dish and strain the sauce over them.

Kidneys and Mushrooms.

Ingredients—2 dozen medium sized mushrooms.

6 sheep's kidneys.

1 pint of second stock.

1 oz. of butter.

1 oz. of flour.

2 tablespoonfuls of cream.

A few drops of lemon juice.

Method.—Peel the mushrooms, cut off the stalks, and wash them.

Wipe the kidneys and slice them, put them in a stewpan with the stock and mushrooms.

Simmer them gently for thirty minutes or more, until quite tender.

Mix the butter and flour very smoothly, stir them in and boil for about three minutes.

Add the cream and let it boil, season to taste, and squeeze in a few drops of lemon juice.

Curried Rabbit.

Ingredients—1 apple.

1 onion.

2 dessertspoonfuls of curry powder.

1½ pint of second stock.

2 tablespoonfuls of cream.

2 oz. of butter.

2 dessertspoonfuls of flour.

Salt.

A few drops of lemon juice.

Method.—Cut the rabbit into neat joints and fry them in the butter.

Then remove them and fry the onion and apple, sliced.

Mix the curry powder and flour smoothly with the stock.

Put it into a stewpan; stir and boil three minutes.

Put in the rabbit and add the onion and apple, which should be rubbed through a hair sieve.

Simmer gently for thirty minutes or more, until the rabbit is tender.

Add the cream and let it boil in the sauce.

Squeeze in the lemon juice and add salt.

If a dry curry is liked, remove the rabbit when tender, and boil and reduce the sauce to half the quantity, leaving only sufficient to coat the pieces of rabbit well.

Serve nicely cooked rice with the curry (*see* Rice for Curry).

Curried Chicken.

Make according to the directions in the preceding recipe, using white stock or boiled milk.

Mutton Cutlets à la Milanaise.

Ingredients—7 or more mutton cutlets.

2 eggs, white bread-crumbs.

3 oz. Parmesan cheese, grated.

A little boiled macaroni.

½ pint brown sauce.

Some mashed potatoes.

2 oz. clarified butter, or the fat skimming of the stock-pot.

Method.—Trim the cutlets neatly.

Brush them with egg and cover them with bread-crumbs mixed with 2 oz. of the grated cheese.

Fry them for about five minutes in a cutlet pan.

6 sheep's kidneys.

1 pint of second stock.

1 oz. of butter.

1 oz. of flour.

2 tablespoonfuls of cream.

A few drops of lemon juice.

Method.—Peel the mushrooms, cut off the stalks, and wash them.

Wipe the kidneys and slice them, put them in a stewpan with the stock and mushrooms.

Simmer them gently for thirty minutes or more, until quite tender.

Mix the butter and flour very smoothly, stir them in and boil for about three minutes.

Add the cream and let it boil, season to taste, and squeeze in a few drops of lemon juice.

Curried Rabbit.

Ingredients—1 apple.

1 onion.

2 dessertspoonfuls of curry powder.

1½ pint of second stock.

2 tablespoonfuls of cream.

2 oz. of butter.

2 dessertspoonfuls of flour.

Salt.

A few drops of lemon juice.

Method.—Cut the rabbit into neat joints and fry them in the butter.

Then remove them and fry the onion and apple, sliced.

Mix the curry powder and flour smoothly with the stock.

Put it into a stewpan; stir and boil three minutes.

Put in the rabbit and add the onion and apple, which should be rubbed through a hair sieve.

Simmer gently for thirty minutes or more, until the rabbit is tender.

Add the cream and let it boil in the sauce.

Squeeze in the lemon juice and add salt.

If a dry curry is liked, remove the rabbit when tender, and boil and reduce the sauce to half the quantity, leaving only sufficient to coat the pieces of rabbit well.

Serve nicely cooked rice with the curry (*see* Rice for Curry).

Curried Chicken.

Make according to the directions in the preceding recipe, using white stock or boiled milk.

Mutton Cutlets à la Milanaise.

Ingredients—7 or more mutton cutlets.

2 eggs, white bread-crumbs.

3 oz. Parmesan cheese, grated.

A little boiled macaroni.

½ pint brown sauce.

Some mashed potatoes.

2 oz. clarified butter, or the fat skimming of the stock-pot.

Method.—Trim the cutlets neatly.

Brush them with egg and cover them with bread-crumbs mixed with 2 oz. of the grated cheese.

Fry them for about five minutes in a cutlet pan.

Dish them on a border of mashed potatoes and put some nicely-cooked macaroni in the centre with 1 oz. of grated cheese.

Pour the brown sauce round them and serve very hot.

Chaud-froid Chicken.

COLD ENTRÉE FOR SUPPERS AND LUNCHEONS.

Ingredients—The best joints of 2 chickens.

1 pint of *Béchamel* sauce.

¼ oz. of Swinborne's or Nelson's Gelatine.

Some aspic jelly.

Endive and lettuce.

Method.—Melt the gelatine and mix it with the sauce.

Coat the pieces of chicken carefully with it, giving them each two coats if they require it.

When the sauce is firm, place them in a circle on an *entrée* dish.

Put some lettuce, nicely mixed with salad dressing, in the centre, and garnish prettily with the endive.

A border of aspic jelly should be placed round the chicken.

If liked, the chicken may be decorated with truffle or ham.

Rissoles of Game.

Ingredients—Some scraps of cold game.

Some very stiff second stock.

Lemon juice, pepper, salt.

Egg and bread-crumbs.

Method.—Mince the game finely.

Melt the stock and moisten the game well with it.

Add pepper and salt, and a few drops of lemon juice.

Spread the mixture on a plate to get cold.

When cold it will be quite firm.

Mould it into balls or egg shapes.

Cover them with egg and bread-crumbs, and fry them in hot fat (*see* French Frying).

Serve on a folded napkin, and garnish with fried parsley.

Podovies.

Ingredients—Some cooked beef, minced finely.

A little thick gravy, lemon juice.

A little pastry.

Pepper and salt.

Some crushed vermicelli and one or two eggs.

Method.—Mix the beef with the gravy; season it with pepper and salt.

Roll out the pastry as thin as possible.

Cut it into rounds with a good-sized cutter.

Brush the edges of the rounds with beaten egg, and put a little of the minced meat in the middle of each.

Fold them over, pressing the edges well together.

Cover with the egg, and then with the vermicelli.

Drop them into hot fat (*see* French Frying) and fry them a golden brown. As they will rise to the top of the fat, it will be necessary to keep them under with a wire basket or spoon. Dish on a folded napkin and garnish with fried parsley.

FISH COOKERY.

To Boil Fish.

Be very careful that the fish is thoroughly cleansed, then place it on the fish-strainer, and tie a cloth, or piece of muslin, over it. (This is to prevent any scum settling on the fish to disfigure it, or spoil its colour.) Immerse it in boiling water, to which two tablespoonfuls of salt, and two of vinegar, have been added; boil it for three minutes to set the albumen on the outside, and so form a casing to keep in the juices and flavour of the fish. Then draw the kettle to the side of the fire and simmer gently until the fish is cooked. For a thick piece of fish, six minutes to each pound, and six minutes over, is the time usually allowed; but no hard-and-fast rule can be laid down, as the time it will take to cook depends on the size and shape, as well as on the weight of the fish. When the fish is cooked, it will have an opaque appearance; and on being pulled, will leave the bone readily. Care must be taken to cook it sufficiently but not to over-boil it. Under-done fish is very unpleasant, while over-cooked fish is flavourless, and breaks to pieces.

Salt fish is put into lukewarm water for the purpose of drawing out some of the salt, and must be simmered until tender. Mackerel should also be put into lukewarm water, as the skin is very tender, and boiling water would break it.

When the fish is cooked, remove the cloth, or muslin, and place the strainer across the kettle that the fish may get well drained. Cover it with a hot cover, and leave it in that position for a few minutes. Then dish, on a folded napkin; or on a strainer, if sauce is poured over it. Garnish tastefully, and serve with an appropriate sauce. Small cod, or salmon, if boiled whole, should be trussed in the form of the letter S.

Baked Fish.

The oven should be kept at a moderate heat, that the fish may not be dried up. Small fish may be cooked with great advantage in the oven, if carefully covered with buttered paper, which will keep them moist, and prevent any baked flavour.

Fried Fish.

Small fish, such as whiting, smelts, &c., are generally fried whole. Larger fish, such as cod and salmon, are fried in the shape of cutlets. Fish to be fried, must be covered with egg and crumbs, or batter. A stewpan, half full of fat, and not a frying-pan, should be used for the purpose (*see* French Frying), except in the case of the sole; and for that, the new fish-fryer, with a wire strainer, is far better than the old-fashioned pan. The bread-crumbs, for fish, should be prepared by rubbing stale bread through a wire sieve.

Boiled Turbot.

Boil it according to the directions for boiling fish. It usually takes from half an hour to an hour, according to its size. It should be dished on a folded napkin, with the white side uppermost; and garnished with cut lemon, parsley, and coral. Serve with it lobster, shrimp, or anchovy sauce.

Boiled Brill.

This fish is cooked like turbot; garnished in the same way, and served with the same sauces.

Boiled Salmon.

Boil according to the directions given for boiling fish. Truss a small salmon in the form of the letter S. Dish on a folded napkin; and garnish with parsley and coral. Serve with lobster, shrimp, anchovy, or tartare sauce.

Boiled Cod.

Boil according to directions given for boiling fish. A small piece is often served with thick egg-sauce poured over it, and garnished with the yolk of an egg rubbed through a wire sieve.

Salt Cod, Haddock, Plaice, and any Fish,

May be boiled according to directions given for boiling fish, and served with egg, anchovy, or any other appropriate sauce.

Curried Fish.

Ingredients—1½ lb. of cold boiled fish.

1 small onion.

1 small apple.

½ pint of second stock.

A few drops of lemon juice.

1 oz. of butter.

1 dessertspoonful of curry powder.

1 dessertspoonful of flour.

Salt.

Method.—Slice the onion and apple; fry them in the butter, and then rub them through a hair sieve.

Mix the flour and curry powder smoothly with the stock.

Stir over the fire and boil well.

Then add the onion, apple, lemon juice, and salt.

Break the fish into pieces, and remove the bones.

Put it into the sauce, and let it warm through.

Serve with a border of rice round it.

Kedgeree.

Ingredients—The remains of cooked fish.

An equal quantity of boiled rice.

2 hard-boiled eggs.

A little butter.

Pepper and salt.

Method.—Break the fish into flakes, removing all the bones.

Melt a little butter in a saucepan.

Put in the rice, fish, and the whites of the eggs cut small, pepper and salt.

Stir over the fire until quite hot.

Heap it on a hot dish in the form of a pyramid, and sprinkle over it the yolks of the eggs, rubbed through a wire sieve.

Baked Herrings.

Ingredients—A few herrings.

Browned bread-crumbs.

A little butter or dripping.

Parsley.

Method.—Split open the herrings, and remove the back-bone.

Roll them up, and place them with their roes on a greased baking-sheet.

Cover them with greased paper, and put them into a moderate oven for ten or fifteen minutes until cooked.

Place the rolls on a folded napkin, and sprinkle some brown bread-crumbs in a straight line on each.

Garnish with the roes and sprigs of parsley.

Herrings baked in Vinegar.

Ingredients—A few herrings.

1 dessertspoonful of finely-chopped parsley.

1 small onion.

Vinegar.

Pepper and salt.

Method.—Grease a pie-dish, and put some herrings at the bottom.

Sprinkle them with the parsley and onion finely chopped, and the pepper and salt.

Put another layer of herrings on the top, and sprinkle them similarly.

Proceed in the same way until the dish is full.

Cover them with vinegar.

Place over them a dish, and bake in a slow oven for three or four hours.

Herrings cooked in this way are used cold.

Smelts Fried.

Ingredients—Smelts.

Egg.

Bread-crumbs.

Parsley.

Method.—Dry the smelts well, and fix their tails in their mouths.

Cover them with egg and bread-crumbs, and fry them a golden brown in a frying-basket in hot fat (*see* French Frying).

Garnish with fried parsley, and serve with melted butter or other suitable sauce.

Smelts au gratin.

Ingredients—Some smelts.

A few button mushrooms.

1 shalot.

1 sprig of parsley.

Lemon juice.

Pepper and salt.

Browned bread crumbs.

Glaze.

Method.—Lay the smelts on a greased baking-sheet.

Sprinkle under and over them the parsley, shalot, and mushrooms, finely chopped, with lemon juice, pepper, and salt.

Cover them with browned bread-crumbs, and put little bits of butter over them.

Bake them in a moderate oven for seven or ten minutes. Put them on a hot dish, and pour melted glaze over them.

Ling and Hake.

These two fish may be cooked according to any of the recipes given for dressing cod.

Salmon à la Tartare.

Ingredients—A piece of salmon.

Some tartare sauce.

Chopped parsley.

Coral.

Method.—Boil the salmon carefully according to the directions given for boiling fish.

Garnish with coral and parsley, and serve with tartare sauce (*see* Sauces).

If the salmon is served cold, the tartare sauce is poured over it. If hot, it is served in a sauce-boat.

A slice of salmon is frequently grilled, and served with tartare sauce.

Pickled Salmon.

Ingredients—Some boiled salmon.

1 dozen peppercorns.

2 saltspoonfuls of salt.

3 bay leaves.

Equal quantities of vinegar and the liquor the fish was boiled in.

Method.—Lay the salmon in a deep pan or pie-dish.

Boil the fish liquor, vinegar, and other ingredients for a quarter of an hour.

Let it get cold, and then pour over the salmon, which should be allowed to remain in the pickle until the next day.

Whitebait.

Ingredients—Whitebait.

Flour.

Method.—Put plenty of oil or fat into a stewpan, and make it hot (*see* French Frying). The heat of the fat for whitebait should be 400°.

Have a good heap of flour on a cloth.

As soon as the fat is hot, throw the whitebait into the flour, and, taking the cloth by each end, shake the whitebait rapidly until they are well floured.

Turn them quickly into a frying-basket.

Shake the basket well for the loose flour to drop off, and throw the whitebait into the fat for a minute.

As soon as they rise to the surface, remove them with a fish-slice, and drain them on kitchen paper.

Serve them with brown bread and butter, and slices of lemon.

www.ingramcontent.com/pod-product-compliance
Lightning Source LLC
Chambersburg PA
CBHW081725100526
44591CB00016B/2501